C000241644

BEAUTY
AND
MEANING

BEAUTY
AND
MEANING

The T. S. Eliot Lectures of the Most Reverend
METROPOLITAN
ANTHONY BLOOM

Foreword by
ROWAN WILLIAMS

EDITED BY JAMES HEYWOOD

DARTON · LONGMAN + TODD

First published in 2023 by
Darton, Longman and Todd Ltd
1 Spencer Court
140 – 142 Wandsworth High Street
London SW18 4JJ

ISBN: 978-1-915412-19-5

A catalogue record for this book is available from
the British Library.

Designed and produced by Judy Linard

Printed and bound in Great Britain by Bell & Bain, Glasgow

TABLE OF CONTENTS

EDITOR'S NOTE

As Metropolitan Anthony mentions in an answer to a question following Lecture 3, when he first came to England in the late 1940s, the little English that he knew had been learned from the Authorised Version of the Bible! The story goes that he actually addressed people as *thou* and *thee* for a time, until he became familiar with modern parlance. That being so, the command of English that he developed as time went on, and which is so evident in these lectures, is quite astounding and wholly admirable.

In addition to his facility with the English language, the references and quotations that he offers during these lectures show his enormous breadth and depth of reading, in English, as well as in Russian, French, German, and possibly other languages too.

Metropolitan Anthony's rich and harmonious voice comes through the recordings of the lectures; those who knew him would recognise his distinct but soft Russian-French accent and his slight lisp. Part of this voice is the few errors he made in speaking English, some of them typical of Russians: maybe an inappropriate choice of tense, a misplaced article, an unusual use of words. It is touching to think that even Metropolitan Anthony was liable to such errors. My approach has been to change as little as possible. Where these small errors do not interfere with the sense, I have let them be, in order to preserve that authentic voice.

Metropolitan Anthony did not read his lectures from a prepared and perfected text; at most he would have some notes as prompts. Anyone who speaks in that way makes small mistakes: unnecessary repetitions, errors in quotations, little stumbles over words. I have taken the liberty of adjusting these to what he either appears to have meant or must have meant to say.

For each of the Metropolitan's citations or quotations, I have added a footnote with information about the person cited or the source of the quotation. Sometimes this has been made difficult by the fact that Metropolitan Anthony was quoting from non-English sources, and often from memory – possibly, in some cases, translating the original himself from his memory of it. (He would have been capable of that.) In addition, Metropolitan Anthony often appears to use quotations in a (shall we say?) creative fashion, adapting the original to his immediate purpose. In such cases, what the Metropolitan says in the lecture may not match any recognised English translation, but I have generally elected to keep his version unchanged, rather than alter the flow of the talk by offering a different text. There is a venerable precedent for this in St Paul's quotations from the Holy Scriptures! Again, the footnotes should guide the reader to the originals.

My Greek definitions are from Liddell and Scott's *Greek-English Lexicon* (1940) or its online manifestation, philolog. us. In tracking down Russian and French quotations and citations I was greatly helped by Elena Sadovnikova, Tatyana Kasatkina and Élie Hériard Dubreuil. I am most grateful to them, and also to David Chambers, who reviewed the edited texts and suggested a number of improvements.

It has been a privilege to edit these lectures by Metropolitan Anthony, whom I remember with great respect and affection. He was a spiritual leader who acquired many disciples because of his wisdom, his integrity, and his ability to express in words, both in Russian and in English, the most profound spiritual and moral truths, in a way that spoke directly to the heart of his listeners. I hope the readers of these lectures may hear him as we heard him in life, and receive at least some of the benefit that we received.

JAMES HEYWOOD
April 2022

FOREWORD

BY ROWAN WILLIAMS

For the countless readers who know Metropolitan Anthony Bloom as a writer on prayer – an exceptionally clear, forceful, humane expositor of the contemplative tradition – this book may come as a surprise. It is a reflection on beauty and meaning, ranging widely in cultural and philosophical territory, displaying a striking familiarity with European, classical and even Asian literature, only seldom venturing into conventionally theological issues. It has all the characteristic strengths of Metropolitan Anthony's writing; it is lively and sometimes witty, relaxed and conversational, but also insistently challenging, even uncompromising. Above all, what it does is to remind us that the serious practice of contemplative prayer involves a sort of cultural revolution: if we learn to pray, we learn to see our human context differently, even to sense our world in a new way. And conversely, when our routine perceptions are interrupted or re-shaped, we are somewhere on the road to prayer, whether or not we know it.

Metropolitan Anthony is sparing in his explicit references to the spiritual tradition that has formed him, but these references are crucial to understanding how his mind works in the lectures printed here. Basic to his approach is a theme that can be found in the classic texts of the *Philokalia*, the great Orthodox collection of authoritative spiritual teaching through the centuries: we see truly and lovingly when we cease to see things or people primarily in relation to ourselves and our needs or dramas. When we are set free from the tangles of fear and greed that get in the way of real openness to what is in front of us, we can find meaning in its most important sense − communicative relationship, the awareness of gifts being offered wherever we look. And any recognition of beauty in the world is a moment of such freedom; we are enabled to see and receive what God gives. In other words, we are being opened up to the dimension of contemplative awareness, which lets us see the world − including our own selves − in relation with God. The deepest form of human failure is the refusal of this and the reduction of what is around us to the demands of the self. We become un-beautiful ourselves and we make the world un-beautiful.

Ugliness, though, has its own role when we have really embarked on the journey of growth towards God. When we recognize our failure, we recognize our weakness, our inability to unite and harmonize the world of our experience – and that recognition itself makes space for God. It reminds us quite simply that God's pervasive agency can do what our human ingenuity cannot. The emphasis on opening our imagination to beauty does not mean that we can never encounter the knowledge that comes only in tragedy. This too has its place in contemplative perception, calling us back to what can be a painful truthfulness about ourselves.

Throughout these lectures, Metropolitan Anthony displays an unfailing honesty in addressing the range of human experience, dark and light; this is no easy recipe for 'aesthetic' spirituality, for the cultivation of exalted and exquisite emotion. His own dictum that we need to get past emotion in order to reconnect with 'feeling' is in the background here: any kind of self-conscious pursuit of sensation will get in the way of plain exposure to what is real – just as any pursuit of 'happiness' will infallibly get in the way of actual joy. With great acumen, he examines the way in which art works – at its truest – to wean us from mere emotion and expose us to the feel of things. The creativity of the artists is always to do with this re-working of the familiar so as to expose the real in the familiar – which means that art consistently makes our world strange to us all over again, makes us learn as if for the first time, and see as if for the first time. The convergence of art with the life of spirit in the fullest theological sense is here, in the laying bare to our senses and our minds of a new creation.

So, while the subject matter of this book appears to be beyond Metropolitan Anthony's usual field of exposition, we are firmly and gently led back to the fundamental spiritual imperatives of his teaching on prayer. And in the process, we are shown, with exceptional skill and range of reference, how the life of prayer is bound up with the creative enterprise in which human beings are always involved. The famous Dostoevskian axiom that 'beauty will save the world' is shown to be more than an appeal to refined perceptions and reactions, or the enjoyment of inspiring or satisfying sensation: for beauty to be 'saving', our hearts and minds need to be stripped and exposed, turned radically away from self-concern. Without this, our awareness of beauty will be no more than another variety of private consolation. But if we can learn the lesson of serious artistic labour, we can begin to see how we can be in deeper communion with what is, how we can find meaning and communication and gift in our world.

These lectures were delivered decades ago, but they have retained their freshness; indeed, our current context, with its deep confusions and anxieties about our relation with an environment wrecked by our inability to see truthfully and relate unselfishly, may find these words echoing with greater urgency than they did even for Metropolitan Anthony's first audiences. They offer

14

FOREWORD

a profoundly valuable bridge between the world of faith
and the world of contemporary thought and perception, a
model of generous, intelligent dialogue.

ROWAN WILLIAMS

LECTURE 1 – MEANING

1 NOVEMBER 1982

I t will be quite obvious to you, having heard the Chairman's introduction, that I have no qualification to give these T. S. Eliot lectures![1] The only direct link I have with Eliot is a conversation I had a few years ago with one of our Orthodox clergy. He strode into my room, holding a book in his hand, looked at me severely, and said, 'I have brought you a book; what happens in it is what will happen to you,' and he made me a present of *Murder in the Cathedral*![2] I am still waiting for the prophecy to be fulfilled, and this is all, really, I can say in my defence in the context of these lectures. Yet, I *am* interested in poetry and in beauty. Ultimately, to me, the name of God is Beauty, and I think that I would agree with a friend of mine, an Orthodox bishop, who said many years ago, 'When God looks at a human being he does not see either achievement or virtues, which may or may not be there, but He sees beauty, which nothing can eradicate.' So

[1]   Thomas Stearns Eliot, OM (1888–1965), born St Louis, Missouri, USA, settled in London in 1914, 'high' Anglo-Catholic essayist, publisher, playwright, literary and social critic, and regarded as one of the twentieth century's major poets.

[2]   T. S. Eliot, *Murder in the Cathedral*, verse drama, first performed in 1935, which portrays the assassination of Archbishop Thomas Becket in Canterbury Cathedral in 1170.

the ultimate meaning of things for me can be defined in terms of beauty, or otherwise of ugliness.

In this first lecture, I want to speak on the subject of 'meaning', because whether we are aware of it, conscious of it or not, we relate to things only to the extent to which they have meaning for us. A totally meaningless thing is something to which we cannot relate. In a way, it is like a language. If we hear a language spoken of which we have no notion, after a while, when we no longer listen to its flow and music, we opt out. So, beauty is an ultimate revelation of things created and of the creator. And meaning is something essential in relation to life in all its forms of expression.

Now, in poetry, or other forms of art, meaning may be at the very centre of things. The poet — and may I remind you that from its Greek roots a poet is a creator[3] — the poet is one who conveys meaning, who makes sense of things, who discloses to us a depth and a significance in things which we, or most of us, are incapable of perceiving: more incapable very often of expressing. This meaning can be conveyed in a variety of ways. It is not only poetry — words, rhythms, sounds, it is not only music — there are many ways in which meaning reaches us. I will give you a few examples.

In the works of the French poet, Victor Hugo,[4] there is

[3] Ποιητής — Greek: maker, inventor, composer (of poem, drama, music), author.

[4] Victor Marie Hugo (1802–1885), poet, novelist, and dramatist of the Romantic movement, considered to be one of the greatest French writers.

a page on which there is only a date, and a dotted line. This is the day when he suffered a bereavement which could not be put into words. It could not be put into sound, it could not be expressed in any way except in silence. And this blank page conveys meaning as much as any words, and more than any words could convey.[5]

There is a story about one of the ancient Persian kings, defeated by a neighbouring potentate. He was made a prisoner, his sons were taken prisoners also, together with many of his family and those around him. His adversary condemned them to death, and to die before the king's eyes. The king wept bitterly. However, when his son was murdered in his presence, he could shed no tear. The tyrant, looking at him, said, 'How deep must be a grief that cannot find even a tear to express it!'[6]

So, that silence, the inability of finding any form

[5]   In 1843, Hugo's eldest and favourite daughter, Léopoldine, aged 19, shortly after her marriage to Charles Vacquerie, drowned in the Seine at Villequier, pulled down by her heavy skirts when their boat overturned. Her young husband also died trying to save her. Her death left her father devastated.

The work cited here is a poem in the collection, *Les Contemplations* (*The Contemplations*, 1856). Its title is the date of Léopoldine's drowning, 4 September 1843, and the poem consists only of a line of dots. The poem is in a section of the collection dedicated especially to Léopoldine, entitled *Pauca Meae*, which may be translated as 'The Little Left to Me'.

[6]   This appears to be a reference to an episode in the *Shahnameh* (Book of Kings), an epic poem written by the Persian poet, Ferdowsi, between 977 and 1010. It consists of 50,000 couplets, telling of the mythical and historical past of the Persian Empire, from the creation of the world until the Arab conquest in the seventh century.

of expression except silence itself, except the statuesque immobility of frozen grief, may convey as much meaning as any word.

I remember someone quoting to me, a few years ago, a short poem by Leonard Cohen,[7] which I do not remember word for word, but the purport of which is:

When I sit silently with you, you say at times,
'It is as beautiful as a poem.'
How I long that one day, when I read one of my poems to you,
you should say, 'It is as beautiful as silence.'[8]

I am insisting on this element of silence, of immobility, of the way in which things do not need a verbal, or noisy, or plastic expression, because it shows how important it is that they reach us as meaning; otherwise there would be no interpretation to any of the examples which I have given.

Meaning is gathered by us from all sorts of aspects of life. But it depends very much on our ability to see, to hear, to perceive, to understand our own experience. We play an active role, both in the perception and in the expression, and if we are too primitive, in the worst sense of the word, if we are incapable of responding to the message which reaches us,

[7] Leonard Norman Cohen (1934–2016), Canadian singer-songwriter, poet and novelist.

[8] Leonard Cohen, 'Gift', from the collection, *The Spice-Box of Earth* (1961).

Lecture 1 – Meaning

or which we are capable of reading in what happens or is outside of us, then we see no meaning. I will give you at least one example.

A few years ago, I was visited by an ecologist, who went around the world asking two questions from people of all walks of life. What he wanted was an immediate response that was not screened through intellectual reflection. It was to be a response, and not the result of a long process of thought. The first question was simple for a clergyman, it was, 'What is silence?' – and you can imagine how much a clergyman can say on silence! But his second question was infinitely more interesting to me. He asked me, 'What is a tree?', and I responded as I could. And then I got very interested, because the response which he had elicited from me was quite different from anything one might expect from someone who was trained in natural sciences, or in medicine, as I am; it had nothing to do with biology. I had just come back from the United States, and had been impressed by the power of that young earth to sprout upwards with such richness, with such greatness, trees, plants, grass; and so I saw a tree as an expression of life, an expression of the life-power of the earth; so I said something briefly about it. But, having got interested, I thought I would ask the same question to those in my surroundings. I selected a young theologian – well-trained, cultured, refined – from whom I expected the most beautiful answer, and a young girl without any particular culture – normal, sane, intelligent – from whom I expected

23

something direct but that would not reach the heights of poetry.

The first one – the cultured, trained, high-minded young theologian – answered my question as to what a tree is by saying, 'A tree? Building material!' The girl, whom I asked what a tree was, said, 'Oh, a tree: it stands for gentleness. Look at the beauty of its crown, look at the movements of its branches and of its leaves; listen to the sound of the breeze and of the rain!' That was a quite different perception. For the first one the tree had no meaning. It was simply an object of self-centred interest. The only thing that interested him in the tree was the way it can be used for his comfort. For the girl, the tree meant something; it conveyed meaning, it had significance. I do not mean, at the moment, to say that all this meaning was within the tree, that it was the tree sharing with this young girl what it perceived of itself, or what it was in substance. But in the relationship that was established between this tree – seen and experienced – and this girl, there was a vision, and that is what we find in poetry.

But meaning is not only in silence, or in this kind of vision: one can find meaning in space.

You remember, probably, that Kant,[9] speaking of aesthetics, said that, ultimately, space and time are the metaphysical substance of aesthetics that is to be brought

---

[9]   Immanuel Kant (1724–1804), German philosopher, founder of the doctrine of Transcendental Idealism.

out. I remember reading a book on architecture, in which the author made it quite clear that what is essential in architecture is not so much the walls, the forms, the shapes, the decoration, but the fact that architecture reveals space. You enter into a limited space and because there is a limit to it, which was created by the vision of someone, space exists and space acquires a meaning, not because of its particular shape, but as such. This is a very important thing, because space may be vast, or it may be small – it may be too small – it has a variety of repercussions on us. Those of you who are interested in Edgar Poe[10] may have read two essays of his on aesthetics. One is called *Landor's Cottage*, and the other *The Domain of Arnheim*. In both essays, Poe measures his vision of space on the scale of man. We will come to this later, but at the moment I want only to point out that, for him, anything which is not on the scale of man is either stifling or terrifying and, therefore, can contain no beauty. And in the two essays he wrote, he tries to describe what an ideal landscape, an ideal *paysage,* scenery is, when it is just on the scale that satisfies, but does not stretch one and, therefore, does not frighten one. To him a thunderstorm, the vastness of the sea or the sky is too much for man and cannot be called beautiful; it is called terrifying; it is dread. Well, here you see that there is this possibility left to each of us to reject a whole world of

---

[10]   Edgar Allan Poe (1809–1849), born Edgar Poe, American writer, editor, and literary critic, best known for his poetry and short stories, particularly his tales of mystery and the macabre.

things, when space is perceived as dread, and not understood, not made into something that makes sense.

Sound also – I am not speaking of music at the moment – but sound, as such, could also be a vector of meaning. There is a whole tradition in the Muslim world of the significance, and the meaning and the use of sound as such, to convey, or to make someone experience or participate in two states of mind, emotions and also spiritual experience as understood by the Sufi, for instance. There is also a very interesting passage in the work of a Jewish writer of the twelfth century, Maimonides (Moses ben Maimon),[11] who, speaking of the way in which we can express the existence of the Person of God, says that the only adequate way to express the ineffable would be to agree that one sound should be singled out and used for nothing other than to indicate that it is of God that one is speaking. It could be a musical note, it could be a combination of sounds, but it should be exclusive. And then it would mean *God*, and contain all the experience that this – not the word, but the Person of God relating to us – means to each person singly, or to mankind or to particular groups collectively.

We find also the same kind of idea in early Siberian tribes, who had this sense of the holiness of God, of his ineffable

[11] Moses ben Maimon, commonly known as Maimonides, born in Córdoba, Almoravid Empire (now part of Spain), 1135 or 1138, died in Egypt, 1204, buried in Tiberias, lower Galilee; Sephardic Jewish philosopher and one of the most prolific and influential Torah scholars of the Middle Ages.

LECTURE 1 – MEANING

quality. There were tribes in which there was no name for God but when, in conversation or in prayer, they wanted either to address him, or signify him, they made a gesture upwards: it meant HIM, nothing more. In Orthodox liturgical practice, there are certain prayers, particularly in the Canon of the Liturgy, in which God is addressed as *Thou*, without any adjective, without any qualification, because this word *Thou* is enough to define the whole range of relationship there is between the person at prayer and God. *Thou* means (in those languages in which it exists, as contrasted with *you*) – *Thou* means, on the one hand, the assertion of a radical otherness (*Thou* means *not I*) and, at the same time, since this word is used only in relation to the closest, the dearest, the nearest, it means a kinship which is beyond any other description.

I am trying to show, or to indicate at least, a variety of ways in which meaning is there in all our vocabulary, in our gestures, in the sounds which we use, in the tone of our voice when we speak to one another, because there is a great deal of difference in the way in which we use a phrase or a word with warmth in our voice and in our heart, or with harshness.

Motion also belongs to this form of expression. That is simpler in a way: who does not know how much can be expressed by the dance in all its aspects or forms, provided this dance comes from within and is not an artificially invented physical exercise: in other words, when it is an expression of things. And the ultimate way in which one can put it is by quoting St Isaac of Syria,[12] a desert hermit of the seventh century in Syria, who said that the dance is the eternal occupation of the angels in heaven. The dance: because the dance contains the totality of contemplative silence and the perfect expression of the inner experience which this silence embodies and which no word can express.

I think I have done with this long list of examples, but I think it is important to realise when we approach poetry, prose, painting, architecture, music – any form of art – that there is always, intentionally or beyond intention, a meaning that is perceived and transmitted, When I say 'intentionally or beyond intention', I mean the following: in one of his letters, Dante,[13] the author of *The Divine Comedy*, says, 'The whole work was undertaken not for a speculative, but for a practical end; to remove those who are living in this life from the state of wretchedness, and to lead them to a state of blessedness.' Here there was a definite intention on Dante's part. He did not write simply because his heart was full and his imagination full of images. He wrote because he perceived the wretchedness,

---

[12]   St Isaac the Syrian (also known as Isaac of Nineveh and Isaac of Qatar), seventh-century Syriac Christian bishop and theologian best remembered for his writings on Christian asceticism. Commemorated (along with St Ephrem the Syrian) on 28 January.

[13]   Durante degli Alighieri, commonly known by his short name Dante Alighieri or simply as Dante (c.1265–1321), Florentine poet, prose writer and political activist. His *Divina Commedia* (*The Divine Comedy*) is widely considered the greatest literary work in the Italian language.

LECTURE 1 – MEANING

the deadly danger in which mankind is placed by its severance from God, by its total misunderstanding of men, by the ways which it has chosen; and it was a cry, a warning, a series of images which were applied to concrete situations, or to concrete persons, but were generalised in such a way that anyone could recognise in one or another situation, in one or another character, something of himself, and receive the warning. It would be superfluous to say that this also was the purpose of the authors of the Gospels when they wrote of Christ. It was not a biography, it was not reminiscences, it was not a treatise on morals but, as St John the Divine[14] says, 'It was all written that we should recognise that Christ is our Saviour and, recognizing this, be saved.'[15]

So, whatever the intention of the author, it reaches us. But there is also so much which in art reaches us almost, as it were, beyond the intention of the author. A cry from the soul, a gesture, which is not intended as a lesson, a teaching, a parable, an allegory or anything, but which comes from within as a necessity, is projected in words, in movement, in line and colour, in sound, or in silence, because the condition of the poet, the creator – in whatever field it is – is such

[14]   St John the Divine, or St John the Theologian, traditionally identified as the beloved apostle, author of the Gospel According to St John, the Epistles of John, and the Book of Revelation; exiled to the island of Patmos during the persecution of Domitian, where he composed Revelation; died in Ephesus *c.* 100. Commemorated 26 September and 8 May.

[15]   *Cf.* John 20:31.

that he cannot keep it to himself. This happens more often probably than the other way around. So many poets have written poetry, so many artists have painted, or composed music, which they re-discovered when they looked at it. I will give you an example which is not of the height of the great poets, and which, again, belongs to the anecdotes of my personal experience.

Some thirty years ago a young man carrying a big object, flat and square, wrapped in a newspaper, came to see me. I had not met him before, so I greeted him and waited. He said to me, 'I am undergoing Jungian[16] analysis. A point has come when my analyst felt that I must begin painting. And I have painted a painting – painted a canvas – but neither I nor the analyst can make any sense of it. I went to see a friend of mine, an elderly lady full of wisdom and goodness, who knows me, and asked whether she could help me. She did not even look at the canvas but she said, "Go and see Father Anthony," (I do not know if she used exactly the same words which he quoted to me, but what he said was) "because he is as mad as you are, and he may be able to read your painting".'

Well, this was the beginning of a comparatively long association. This painting was immensely interesting. It was a totally black background with just a dot of beautiful blue in a corner. To begin with I saw nothing. So I asked him

[16]   Carl Gustav Jung (1875–1961), Swiss psychiatric practitioner and founder of analytical psychology.

to leave the painting with me, in the hope that time would lend it some meaning. I sat for three or four days, seeing people, talking to people, but with the painting in front of me. Gradually I discovered that the painting was not black, it was dark green, and it was not uniform; it was made of waves. And when I had looked long enough, I discovered that all the waves were like a sea in a storm, but all the sea in the storm ended by becoming the face of Mephistopheles, with two hands held about this tiny speck of beautiful, azure light. When I told him that, he said, 'I see!' The next step was for him to say, 'But is it not that there is still in me a spark of heaven and of light, which is endangered by all the darkness and all the storm there is in me?' Well, at that point I left him to his psychoanalyst! But after that a series of paintings emerged, which were as obscure to him and his analyst as the first, and for several months I went to see his paintings, sat in front of them and tried to receive an impact, and then responded. And then he began to read himself into the painting, which had been projected out of him, beyond his conscious intention of expressing what he now read.

The same happens, as far as I am aware, with certain poets or writers who, taken in the grip of an experience, express it, possessed, almost – in the strong sense of the word – possessed by a feeling of something which is beyond the realm of their clear consciousness.

Now, obviously, the simplest way of interpreting it is psychoanalysis: is by saying, 'Well, they have projected out of their sub-conscious what their clear conscious did not know.' This we will have to examine a little more because it may be partly true, but it certainly is only very partly true, though there is definitely truth in it. All the experience of Jungian analysis of painting shows it but, for the moment, let me say this: supposing that it was a projection of self – which self? It is certainly not the superficial self of awareness and consciousness. It may be the self of the sub-conscious; it may be something more than this. The German writer, Nietzsche,[17] wrote that we should beware lest we imagine that our nature is all within us. He says, 'Remember that your nature is beyond you, above you.' And what we can express is perhaps far more than what is contained within us, either personally, individually or ancestrally.

All this could be summed up in a phrase written by a French aestheticist called Étienne Souriau,[18] who says that 'the power to make goes beyond thought and dream.'

This sums up what I have said, in the sense that the power to make, the ability which is that of a poet – understood in the general sense of ποιητής – the ability which the poet has to express an experience of the surrounding world goes beyond

---

[17] Friedrich Wilhelm Nietzsche (1844–1900), German philosopher, cultural critic, composer, poet, philologist, and Latin and Greek scholar whose work has exerted a profound influence on Western philosophy and modern intellectual history.

[18] Étienne Souriau (1892–1979), French philosopher, Professor of Aesthetics at the Sorbonne.

LECTURE 1 – MEANING

what he can dream of it, or what he can think of it. There is a direct, immediate perception which is in the realm of intuition. In that sense for instance you can find a description of it, of this direct, intuitive perception in *The Cocktail Party*. Towards the end, a character called Reilly says:

> *When I first met Miss Coplestone, in this room,*
> *I saw the image, standing behind her chair,*
> *Of a Celia Coplestone whose face showed the astonishment*
> *Of the first five minutes after a violent death.*
> *If this strains your credulity, Mrs. Chamberlayne,*
> *I ask you only to entertain the suggestion*
> *That a sudden intuition, in certain minds,*
> *May tend to express itself at once in a picture.*
> *That happens to me, sometimes. So, it was obvious*
> *That here was a woman under sentence of death.*
> *That was her destiny.*[19]

This could not be expressed more clearly. Intuition: an intuition means a perception which is not built on a rational analysis, which is not the result of a progressive analysis of data which, afterwards, are brought together in a synthesis. A French logician[20] described the rational process by saying, 'It can be summed up by saying, "Oh – but – if – yet – oh

---

[19]   T. S. Eliot, *The Cocktail Party* (1948), scene 3.

[20]   It has not been possible to identify this logician.

– therefore" ', and this is not the way in which either a poet can discover a piece of poetry within himself, or an architect or a painter project his experience. Some do. I remember the Russian abstract painter, Lanskoy,[21] who died in Paris a few years ago, who spent days and days composing an abstract painting. He would sit for hours and hours building it out of rational elements which he wanted to convey. When I asked him whether, when it was finished, it was understood, he said, 'No!' Abstract things – paintings or models – are a language which one man can speak, two or three, perhaps, can understand. But this is the point at which the rational working-out made it impossible for others to have access, because between the direct intuition which could be projected on canvas and which could be received back in the same intuitive way, there was a rational process which distorted the experience by making it rational instead of direct.

All this, really, is aimed at insisting – insisting perhaps too heavily – on the fact that whatever comes out of a creator is to be understood. It can be understood directly and intuitively; it can be understood in a complex process of intuitive perception and reflection. But it cannot be left without meaning and, certainly, if a piece of creation has no meaning whatever, or if its meaning is such that it cannot reach anyone, it is wasted. It is wasted not only for the person who could

[21] André Lanskoy (1902–1976), Russian painter and printmaker who worked in France. He is associated with the School of Paris, and Tachisme, an abstract painting movement that began during the 1940s.

LECTURE 1 – MEANING

receive the message; it is wasted for the person who gave the message. Because someone who speaks a language which no one understands, tries to convey meaning by means which no one will be able to understand, falls short of his own essential intention of communicating. One could apply here a phrase which a French writer, Édouard Estaunié,[22] wrote in one of his novels called *Malaisie*.[23] There is a character who is asked what is his aim in life, what does he wish to achieve in his life? And his answer is, 'To posit, to make quicker than thought an action that would be certainty in itself.' And a piece of art is, in that respect, certainty, and it is an action: not the result of a long process of intentional working, but an action which perhaps goes beyond the very understanding, the very knowledge of the creator; which requires the co-operation of the creator with the person and the persons who will look at the object. It may be one person, it may be a generation of people, it may be centuries, because you are well aware that in our experience of art there are centuries of art with which we are confronted, and every century responds differently to the art of a previous epoch, of a previous situation.

The forms are very often – more often than not – determined by time, by the epoch, by the surroundings, by human characteristics, historical events; but the content, if

[22] *Édouard Estaunié* (1862–1942), French novelist.

[23] Perhaps Metropolitan Anthony means Estaunié's novel, *L'infirme aux mains de lumière* (1923), rather than *Malaisie* (1931), which is by Henri Fauconnier.

it is truly art and not simply a copy of outward reality, is something that reaches us through centuries. If we take the statues or the architecture of ancient Greece, if we take the great pieces of art of all the countries and civilizations, we may feel that we would not express things in these particular terms, we would not use this technique to express perspective, we would not use these colours, or these lines, we would not use these conventions whether verbal, or pictorial, or musical; but we could express the same thing in our own way. And this is brought out very clearly in the fact that we have so many variations written by one composer on the work of another composer: he listened, received a message, transmuted it within himself, in his own terms; but it is the same message seen by another man, received into another soul (I am using the word 'soul' for lack of a better expression) and re-conveyed in new terms. This is something that happens in all forms of art.

Obviously, there are also people who try to reproduce the kind of reality which is around them, who are mere copyists, but this is not art. If it is used and exploited for extraneous purposes, it is even less art. It may convey thoughts or emotions which are alien to the aim of the designer or the painter, in which case one must ask oneself moral questions. I will give you an example and I hope I will not offend anyone. If you go along the streets of a city, or in the Underground, you cannot help seeing a variety of posters advertising a variety of products. No poster says,

LECTURE 1 – MEANING

'Buy cigarettes', 'These cigarettes are good', or 'Buy such and such product'. There will be scenery which will induce in you a mood of serenity, of peace, of calm, of beauty (in very inverted commas!) and then, in a corner, a packet of cigarettes and, smaller than that, the price. The purpose of it all is to attract your attention and to create in you the sense of, 'Oh, how lovely it would be in this background', and then to say, 'And how much more lovely to be there with a cigarette.' The same would be true for all sorts of advertising and expressions. There are posters which border on the pornographic, there are some which make use of great paintings, prostituting greatness to very mercantile intentions. But that is not art. Why? Not because what is seen is bad, but because it is a lie. The intention is not to reveal beauty; the intention is to lure us through beauty, through an emotion, to something which has nothing to do with it. The same would be true with attempts at painting or literature, the aim of which would be nothing, nothing but to give a sort of superficial pleasure – what Dostoyevsky[24] calls 'titillation of the senses'.

---

[24] Fyodor Mikhailovich Dostoyevsky (1821–1881), Russian novelist, short story writer, essayist, journalist and philosopher, whose writings explore human psychology in the troubled political, social and spiritual environment of nineteenth-century Russia, engaging with various philosophical and religious themes. A devout Orthodox Christian, he was a traditionalist and a pacifist, and extolled Christianity as the solution to political and social problems.

There is a phrase of Pascal[25] which I find very interesting: 'How vain is the painting which calls out admiration by the resemblance which it has to things of which we never admire the originals'[26] – a painting which does not reveal the meaning of something so that afterwards we will recognise meaning in what we see, but one which creates an entity that bears the same name as a real object, but which screens away the object, which makes the object unnecessary.

So one can say that any creator, in all the ways and forms of art, is one who receives a message, who transmutes the message within himself into a form (it may be silence, gesture, word, sound, etc.) and who conveys it so that it becomes accessible to others. It's a man who has vision and who sees not the externals, which anyone can see (wood is building material) but who, beyond the visible, sees something more. When I say 'more' I am just being careful, because I do not mean that he sees the essential nature, the substance, the *esse* of things. His vision may be limited, his vision may be more or less distorted by what he is and by his capabilities, but he has seen something in depth. And why? Because he has looked at things not from his point of view but from the point of view of a visionary and, if I may

[25] Blaise Pascal (1623–1662), French mathematician, physicist, inventor, writer and Roman Catholic theologian.

[26] Adapted from Pascal, *Pensées.*

be allowed five more minutes, I would like to give you a couple of examples.

Professor Vysheslavtsev,[27] a Russian philosopher of our century, in his introduction to a book on mystical prayer called *The Way of a Pilgrim*,[28] says, 'What is the difference between the vision of this pilgrim and the vision of the peasant when they look at the same surrounding world? The difference,' he says, 'lies in the fact that the peasant looks at the earth and gauges what it can bring forth in terms of a harvest. The visionary, the mystic, the poet looks at it and sees it for what it is without any reference to himself, without calculation, without trying to see what can be got out of it. He does not read himself into it, he looks at it and receives a message.' The kind of message he receives we will come to in my following talks.

Now, another example can be taken – and I apologise to those of you who know me well and have heard me quote

---

[27] Boris Petrovich Vysheslavtsev (1877–1954), Russian philosopher and religious thinker. Expelled from the Soviet Union in 1922, he became a professor at the Orthodox Theological Institute of St Serge in Paris, was associated with Nikolai Berdyaev and was active in the ecumenical movement. Died in Switzerland.

[28] *The Way of a Pilgrim*, nineteenth-century Russian work (original title: Откровенные рассказы странника духовному своему отцу – *Candid Narratives of a Pilgrim to His Spiritual Father*), recounting the narrator's journey as a mendicant pilgrim through Ukraine, Russia, and Siberia while practising the Jesus Prayer. Discovered at a monastery on Mount Athos in Greece and first published in Kazan in 1884.

these examples before – can be taken from Charles Williams.[29] In *All Hallows' Eve*[30] he describes the fate of a girl who has died in a brutal accident. She has never been aware of anyone, or anything, but herself, and, when she is deprived of her body – when there is left of her nothing but a soul and therefore she cannot relate physically to the surrounding world – she is in an emptiness, she sees nothing. Then gradually she begins to relate to one thing or another and, at a certain moment, she finds herself on the banks of the River Thames. She looks at this river. Before, when she was possessed of a body she recoiled from it because she saw in it the dirty, polluted, greasy waters carrying the refuse of the big city of London, and she reacted to it, as it were, by thinking, 'Oh, God forbid that I should drink of this water, that I should be plunged into it'. But now she has no body that can elicit a reaction of that kind, and so she looks at it and sees the River Thames for a fact, for what it is, and it is totally adequate to what the River Thames, running through London, should be. And because she accepts – totally, unreservedly – the Thames for what it is, through a first layer of opacity and pollution she begins to see successive layers of lesser opacity, of lesser pollution, then a depth where the water is clear, then a depth where the water is pure – the primeval waters which God created – and, at the

[29] Charles Walter Stansby Williams (1886–1945), British poet, novelist, playwright, theologian and literary critic.

[30] Charles Williams, novel, *All Hallows' Eve* (1945).

heart of these waters, a glittering, a brilliant stream of water in which she recognises the water which Christ gave to the Samaritan Woman.[31]

Well, this is a process perhaps – immediate, obviously not dialectical – through which reality can be perceived by a poet: a vision that is possible because, at least at that particular moment, he is free of self; or, if he is involved, he is not involved in terms that make the surrounding world as small as he is but that allow him to expand to the scale of what he sees. There is disinterestedness, there is freedom, there is a communion in intuition that is at the heart of this poetic or creative process.

I will continue to speak a little on these lines next time when I engage in the first of my two talks on beauty, and then I will come to a subject which may seem absurd to many, but which I believe should be looked at: the meaning of ugliness – not the fact of it; that is simple – but its place, its role, its significance.

Thank you for being patient and listening so long.

[31] See the account of Christ's encounter with the woman of Samaria, John 4:5–42, particularly v14.

QUESTIONS

Would you say that the vision that that girl has in All Hallows'
Eve *about the Thames is roughly the same as, say, a devout Hindu
has about the Ganges?*

This is not an easy question to answer. First, I have not
experienced what Lester[32] experienced, and I have not
experienced what a Hindu does. But I think there is a
difference. I think, in the mind of Charles Williams, the
intention was to show that the moment we can disentangle
ourselves from selfish, or self-centred, attitudes to what
surrounds us, we can see things as they are, whatever there
is in them: it could be purely natural things, or supernatural
ones. While a Hindu, as far as I am aware from reading – and
perhaps many of you may put me right – a Hindu treats the
Ganges as a sacrament: as something which is holy in itself
and which, therefore, cannot be penetrated. A sacrament in
Greek is called *mysterion*, a mystery.[33] We are used to using
the word 'mystery' to signify something which we cannot
understand, which is veiled, which is hidden from us. We
say, 'a mysterious visitor': someone about whom we know
nothing. But the word comes from the Greek word which

---

[32]   Lester Furnival, protagonist of Charles Williams' *All Hallows' Eve*.

[33]   Μυστήριον – Greek: secret rite (as in plural. mysteries), objects used
in mysteries, secret, secret revealed by God, i.e. religious or mystical truth.

means 'to be silent, to be spellbound', to be confronted with a reality which is beyond intellection, but not beyond communion with it. I think this is the attitude of a Hindu with regard to the Ganges, or to a piece of blessed bread, the *prasad*, which would be offered and received as a mystery, as something which is loaded with content, which can be shared perhaps to the extent to which you are receptive, but which cannot be analysed because it is transcendental in itself. But this is my reaction to a question which I have never asked myself, and the elements of which I may not possess.

ℛ

You spoke, Archbishop, of our reaction to art as being both intuitive and rational. Do you feel that those two responses are in any way mutually exclusive?

No: I am quite certain they are not mutually exclusive. For a piece of art to be understood, lived with, perceived, there must be both. Because our rational approach is always on the scale of our rational capabilities, whereas our intuition may widen, sort of break our limits, and make it commune with something which is greater than us.

I am struck by the way in which psychoanalysts have examined paintings. I remember Freud[34] making an analysis

---

[34] Sigmund Freud, born Sigismund Schlomo Freud (1856–1939), Viennese neurologist and Jung's rival as the founder of psychoanalysis.

43

of a painting of St Anne, which is in the Louvre.[35] Well, to
– shall I say? – to any ordinary person it is a very beautiful
painting, representing St Anne. But he looked at it long
enough to see in the drapery of her clothes a vulture; and,
from there, he builds a whole conception of a psychoanalysis
both of the object – that is St Anne – and of the painter. I
have nothing to say about it: the only thing is that there is for
me an interrogation mark!

I could give you other examples. It has been said by
another psychoanalyst (I cannot remember now who) that
Utrillo's[36] concentration on painting pubs and cafés was a way
of sublimating his desire to get drunk. Well, maybe! It has
been said by psychoanalysts that Goethe[37] wrote his *Werther*[38]
to sublimate his desire to commit suicide. Maybe! But this
is something which, to me, one reads into a text starting

[35]   Leonardo da Vinci, *The Virgin and Child with Saint Anne*, oil on wood,
painted about 1503.

[36]   Maurice Utrillo, born Maurice Valadon (1883–1955), French painter
who specialised in cityscapes.

[37]   Johann Wolfgang von Goethe (1749–1832), German novelist,
poet, dramatist, autobiographer, literary and aesthetic critic, scientist,
and statesman at the princely court of Weimar. He exerted a profound
influence on the art and science of the nineteenth century, across Europe
and America. Matthew Arnold called him 'the clearest, the largest, the
most helpful thinker of modern times'.

[38]   *The Sorrows of Young Werther* (*Die Leiden des jungen Werthers*, 1774),
loosely autobiographical epistolary novel, which established Goethe's
reputation at the age of 24. Its protagonist, Werther, kills himself to
resolve a love triangle. Goethe asserted that he 'shot his hero to save
himself'.

with premises, starting with the conviction that, if one sort of makes a post-mortem of a piece of art, one will read into it a great deal which may be there or not: which cannot be proved. But I do not think this is a way of appreciating art. I do not know whether anyone of you has read what Jung, for instance, or Lipps[39] or Göring[40] have written on art from the point of view of psychoanalysis. A piece of art appears to be nothing but the expression of mental, emotional processes – either disturbed or less disturbed – of the artist; but there is nothing beyond it. The piece of art is a facet of the artist and our enjoyment in it – and that is either Lipps' or Göring's point of view – is our enjoyment of ourselves when we see ourselves posited in front of us. To me it is very much like the story of Narcissus, who looked at himself and found himself so beautiful that he died of it. And we may well die inwardly if we see nothing but ourselves in the pieces of art with which we are confronted.

Now, this is something which we can easily fall a prey to by analysing intellectually a piece of art and losing what the artist irrationally put into it. 'Irrationally' does not mean unreasonably or foolishly; it means that what he did was beyond him: he saw more than he imagined he saw. There is, in a Russian writer

[39]   Theodor Lipps (1851–1914), German philosopher.

[40]   Matthias Heinrich Göring (1879–1945), German (Nazi) psychiatrist, cousin of Hermann Göring, head of the German General Medical Society for Psychotherapy and director of the Berlin Psychoanalytic Institute/German Institute for Psychological Research and Psychotherapy.

called Gogol,[41] a passage in which a character says: 'The soul of Katerina knows more than Katerina knows.'[42] Well, there is something of that kind in the artist who creates; he creates beyond himself. I do not mean in a state of ecstasy as described, say, in the lives of saints, but in a state of perceptiveness that is beyond his habitual normal condition. It is not the same man who, at another moment, is cross because his shaving water is too cold; it is not the same man who is pernickety about his lunch; it is not the same man who is a fop in the way he dresses: there is a moment when all that vanishes because he has seen something so significant but he could not analyse it. When you think, for instance, of van Gogh's *Olive Orchard in San Rémy*:[43] if you were confronted with the orchard, the orchard would be in front of you, and you would be examining it. When you are confronted with the painting, *you* are in front of the painting: then it is the painting that takes hold of you – and not you of the orchard – and that because between you and the orchard someone has seen a sort of essence, something substantial about it that was conveyed, which was neither stems, nor leaves nor

[41]   Nikolai Vasilievich Gogol (1809–1852), Russian dramatist, novelist and short-story writer, considered by his contemporaries to be one of the pre-eminent figures of the natural school of Russian literary realism.

[42]   Gogol, *A Terrible Vengeance* (Страшная месть), short story, published in the collection, *Evenings on a Farm near Dikanka* (Вечера на хуторе близ Диканьки ,1832).

[43]   Metropolitan Anthony is probably referring to *Olive Trees with the Alpilles in the Background*, painted by van Gogh at the asylum in St Rémy in 1889, now in the Museum of Modern Art, New York.

olives: it was an orchard, a way in which olive trees – of which each has got something to say – relate to the total orchard and to each other and, therefore, can have an impact on you.

ᔓ

Are your comments on 'Meaning' and 'Beauty' informed, could we say, by the iconographic tradition of the Orthodox Church?

I wish they were! I wish I was knowledgeable enough and perceptive enough of the iconographic tradition to be able to see things from within it. I know something about icons, and I will try say something about them. I receive a message from icons but I think there is space in art for things which are not icons. Icons are a message of a certain type about the world in which we live. But it is not the whole world in which we live and, in that sense, one could even say there is even more than the icon concerning what message the icons have to give.

If I may put it in a parallel: there is nothing greater in the experience of a Christian than Holy Communion; yet, after the Communion of priests and people, the priest says in a prayer, 'Lord, grant us to commune even more truly unto Thee in Thy Kingdom which is to come.'[44]

---

[44] This is one of a set of prayers said privately by the priest or deacon after receiving Holy Communion. The set comprises the troparion, 'We have seen the Resurrection of Christ,' which is sung after the reading of the Gospel during Sunday Matins, followed by the irmos and troparia of the 9th Ode of the Canon of Pascha, of which this is the 2nd troparion: 'O Great and most Sacred Pascha, Christ, Wisdom and Word and Power of God, Grant us to partake of you more fully in the day without evening of your Kingdom.'

47

BEAUTY AND MEANING

Even if the icon is a window on eternity, there is an eternity which is beyond the icon. If I may put it in an image, the image of a stained-glass window: We cannot see light, the light which surrounds us, which reveals to us everything around us, but which is revealed in a way by nothing. A stained-glass window, because it is made of so many colours and has a theme, reveals two things to us immediately: by the theme it tells us a story, something, say, about the life of Christ, or a saint, or an event; by its colour it conveys to us this story with the intensity of beauty. But when we have seen and understood both the theme and the beauty, we must remember that both the theme and the beauty are revealed to us by the light which is beyond. And this, I think, would apply to icons. But if we have learnt through the contemplation of icons, through the understanding of what an icon stands for, to see the world in terms of icons, then we must turn to the surrounding world and, in the twilight which the world represents, is or lives in, learn to discern not the darkness, but the light. I would quote here what I have said before: the Orthodox bishop who said, 'When God looks at a person, or at mankind, He does not see the virtues, or the achievements, which are not there; he sees the beauty which nothing can erase.'

LECTURE 2 – BEAUTY – PART 1

2 NOVEMBER 1982

I look with surprise at the audience because I expected an empty hall!

I would like to start with an apology, or a correction of what I said yesterday. When I gave examples of seeing an object without meaning, and seeing meaning in an object, I spoke of a young theologian who had defined a tree in terms of 'building material'. And I was rightly reproached afterwards by someone who remarked that it is not fair on men who work in wood, or in metal, or in other materials, to imagine that they see nothing of beauty in the material which they handle. Indeed, it was none of my intention, but what I wanted to convey was that a man, who works in wood or in metal, and creates an object in the process of his work, can also appreciate the nature of the material which he works upon; he can perceive wood in all its richness; while a young man who, confronted with the thought of a tree sees nothing but 'wood', not what can be created out of it, but merely building material, falls short of a vision. If you want an image more adequate than the one I gave yesterday, you could go to the Dickensian[45] character who, seeing oxen

---

[45]   Charles John Huffam Dickens (1812-1870), English writer and social critic. He created some of the world's best-known fictional characters, and increased his fame iinternationally by giving public readings of his works.

in the market, exclaimed, with elation, with gastric enthusiasm, 'Live beef! Live beef!'[46] I think that is really a more appropriate image, and it is very much what I meant to convey.

Now, it is of beauty that I should speak today, and no longer on meaning specifically.

There is an old saying, at least as old as Goethe,[47] that 'Beauty is in the eye of the beholder.' One could also say that beauty and ugliness are in the eye of the beholder. But does it mean that there is nothing outside of the beholder which calls for the name, 'beauty'? On the other hand, also, how does a person who sees beauty, or who sees an object outside of himself, recognise or identify beauty in it? Well, it is a question of the way we relate to the object. In that respect the ancient thinkers, beginning with, or perhaps rather including Plato,[48] thought of beauty in terms of cognition and not of aesthetic delight. Beauty was a way of entering into a sort of communion with an object that presents itself to us.

[46] Charles Dickens, *Mr Pickwick's Story*, from *Master Humphrey's Clock*, a collection originally published in weekly instalments. The character is called John Podgers.

[47] See footnote 44, Lecture 1.

[48] Plato (428/427 or 424/423 – 348/347 BC), philosopher in Classical Greece and founder of the Academy at Athens, the first institution of higher learning in the Western world: widely considered the pivotal figure in the development of Western philosophy.

The French philosopher, Lévy-Bruhl,[49] said that to recognise beauty is to enter into mystical participation with the object in which we do recognise it – in other words, which we recognise as beautiful. It is knowledge of communion which can be interpreted in different ways. It may be that we read into the object a beauty or something which is within us. It may also be that the object presents us with a character to which we are bound to respond by recognizing beauty. The first type of approach, the reading into an object of characters which are human, that is the humanizing of an object, can be seen (I am speaking more broadly for a moment than of beauty alone) in the way in which we would say that an animal is an embodiment of a given quality: the way in which we make an allegory of an animal. When we say, looking at a hyena, 'Oh, this is a nasty, furtive and ferocious animal!' it does not imply that we know anything about hyenas but, seeing the way in which it trots along, seeing that its foreparts are higher than the hinder parts, seeing the expression on its face, we think, 'Oh, if any of my relations, or friends, or acquaintances had a face like this, a gait like that, moved in that particular way, what a nasty creature he would be!' And the poor hyena is stamped a nasty creature!

The same, perhaps in a more refined way, is said by some

---

49 Lucien Lévy-Bruhl (1857–1939), French philosopher and anthropologist, who contributed to the budding fields of sociology and ethnology, primarily in the study of primitive mentality. His work influenced the psychological theory of Jung.

psychoanalysts, who hold that we speak of beauty in terms of empathy; in other words, of looking at an object and of pouring ourselves into it, and then looking again and seeing ourselves – to use a horrible expression – 'objectivised' (it is an expression of Göring[50]), objectivised outside of ourselves and responding – that is seeing how beautiful *we* are!

There is also a process which was described by other psychoanalysts who studied art. They speak of giving a soul to an object, and thereby affirm, not only by implication but explicitly, that no object has a content in itself that can reach us: that it is we who give a soul to it, a significance to it, and then read it in a second process – as it were, in a second move.

There can also be another approach, held by a great many ancient and modern writers, that there is indeed something outside of us which can be termed beauty or ugliness, and I will try gradually to disentangle, if not *your* thoughts, at least *mine* about it in the process of this talk and the next one.

There is certainly an element which can be expressed in the terms of Goethe. Yes, beauty is in the eye of the beholder, because the beholder must be capable of seeing, and it is not everyone who is capable of seeing. (When I use the word, 'see', I mean 'perceive' in all possible ways. It would take too long to say every time 'to see, to hear, to

---

[50] See footnote 40, Lecture 1.

smell and so forth'.) I will give you an example of this, taken from Persian literature.

There was in ancient Persia a very well-known and revered poet called Majnun,[51] and he spent his life writing most lyrical poems about his beloved one, who was called Layla. So beautiful were the poems, and so beautiful was Layla in the poems, that the Shah decided that he must see the object of all this poetry. Layla was brought to him and, using his prerogative as a ruler, he commanded her to take off her veil, and then he shrank away; because (as the description goes) her nose was like the trunk of an elephant, her mouth like that of a camel, her ears like those of a donkey … the original description is much richer and more convincing than anything I can do! Then the Shah looked at Majnun and said, 'But Majnun, she is horrid! How can you say that she is beautiful?' And Majnun answered, 'You must have the eyes of Majnun to be able to see Layla.'

Of course, this may be called a caricature; you may say that it is impossible to speak in such terms. However, I would say it is not only possible: it happens all the time. It is enough

---

[51] *Layla and Majnun* or *Leili o Majnun* is a narrative poem by the twelfth-century Persian poet, Nizami Ganjavi. It is based on a semi-historical Arab story about the seventh-century Bedouin poet, Qays ibn Al-Mulawwah, and his ladylove, Layla bint Mahdi (or Layla al-Aamiriya). In the poem, Qays and Layla fall in love but are not allowed to marry. Qays becomes obsessed with Layla, and his tribe gives him the epithet, Majnun ('crazy', literally 'possessed by Jinn'). After many trials, Layla dies of grief, Qays rushes to her grave and dies there, and they are buried side by side. Byron called the poem 'the *Romeo and Juliet* of the East.'

for one of us to love another person to be able to see beauty where someone else does not see it. This beauty which we see, is there, only we do not attach the term of beauty to the particular feature of a face or to the structure of a body. We perceive, as it were in transparency, the shining of a personality. In that respect, if we speak of beauty in terms of cognizance, of knowledge, of knowing, we must realise that it is not indifferent whether we look at an object with one attitude of mind or another. Total indifference does not allow us to see either beauty or ugliness. An attitude of mind that would say, 'I do not care at all what this object is', lends us no secret concerning this object. Hatred and love can, but they offer, they disclose to us either beauty or ugliness, not indifferently – that is with reactions which are not indifferent. Hatred singles out all that can be used for criticism, for rejection, to recoil away from an object. In the same line as hatred, one would include fear or any of the negative attitudes to a person or to an object. On the other hand, love, which is openness, trustfulness, confidence – at times a confidence and a trustfulness which is prepared to go to the extreme and take all risks, rather than shut itself up – can reveal to us beauty.

We respond most of the time to circumstances, to people or to beings, in very personal terms. We respond to people according to what they represent for us in terms of risk or of elation, of blossoming out or, on the contrary, of recoiling. Faced with an object of danger we have no time, but also even less inclination to see whether it is beautiful or not. We see only the elements which we would term ugly, to use a very general expression. But when we look at the same object with a sense of security, then we can discern beauty.

Confronted with, say, a wild animal, or with a violent person, in a situation in which we can become the victims of danger, we will see only what is negative. Confronted with the same being in a position of safety we can see beauty, harmony. If any of us had to face a live tiger that had escaped from a cage, we would not have time or inclination to analyse the beauty of the animal, the elegance of its motion, or to appreciate with what purposefulness the animal crouches down ready to jump. Why? Because the centre of gravity would be in us, not at all in the animal.

On the contrary, when the animal is safely in a cage, we would just melt seeing the beauty of its fur; we would admire its teeth, we would look at its paws and the powerful claws, and perhaps even sing the praises of God who has created something so purposeful. The only thing is that then we think that its purpose is not directed at us, but at some other victim.

I remember the story of a group going on safari and being warned not to open windows, not to open the top of the car, not to look out of the doors because, said the guide, 'You must remember that to the animals that will surround you, you are nothing but "meals on wheels"!'[52]

---

[52] 'Meals on Wheels': a social or charitable service provided in the United Kingdom, whereby hot meals are brought to old or disabled people in their own homes.

Well, to be meals on wheels is something that does not inspire us to be serene and contemplative – to be detached in the sense that I tried to point out yesterday. But it is when we are capable of contemplation, of vision, that we can acquire this detachment of communion which is described in so many ways. I have not the time, I think, to make quotations; perhaps if I finish early I will quote to you a short poem of the German writer Hugo von Hofmannsthal,[53] to show you how serenity can be possessed by one who looks at a scene, at a situation, without being involved and can really see it as a glorious harmony. This means that the contemplation of beauty, the ability to perceive beauty, is one of the ways in which (to use the imagery of Schopenhauer[54]) we can overcome a sort of wild lust for life and acquire a serenity which does not detract anything from the intensity, but annihilates the brutality of the predatory way in which we so often treat life and our neighbour.

Beauty has been defined by people who could look serenely at things, beings – human or animal – around them, even at the phenomena of nature like a storm, a thunderstorm, an earthquake, or anything to which we react in such ambiguous and different ways. Beauty has been defined as the convincing power of truth. Truth has beauty in itself. And if something, which is a truth, or true, does not

---

[53] Hugo von Hofmannsthal (1874–1929), Austrian writer and librettist.

[54] Arthur Schopenhauer (1788–1860), German philosopher.

reach us in terms of harmony and beauty it remains exterior to us, alien to us, and very often is not even seen as being truth. Considering this, I think one can say that art in all its forms participates in this complex reality of beauty as being the power of truth.

A number of years ago an English mathematician called Hardy[55] wrote a book on the beauty of mathematics. Now, he obviously did not write of things as simple as '2 plus 2 makes 4 and always 4', but of higher mathematics in which the solution of a complex problem reaches a point which is harmony, which is an equivalence between the various elements of reality. But if you think of its being possible for mathematics to be seen in terms of beauty (because beauty would be defined as serene and final harmony, as a perfect equilibrium of things), we must realise that mathematics – that is number, space, time – is implicit in more than the mathematician's or the physicist's research. Music can be studied in mathematical terms. A sound can always be expressed in terms of vibrations, in terms of waves, in terms which can be shown either by mathematical figures or mathematical design, curves and so on.

There is a very interesting study that was made some years

---

[55]   Godfrey Harold 'G. H.' Hardy, FRS (1877–1947), English mathematician, known for his achievements in number theory and mathematical analysis; also remembered for his 1940 essay on the aesthetics of mathematics, entitled *A Mathematician's Apology*.

ago, on the Cathedral of Chartres,[56] in which an architect and other people studied the cathedral's structure and discovered that the whole cathedral is built on several elements: first of all, on a square, secondly on a five-pointed star – the square representing a complete stability and harmony, and the five-pointed star being a symbol of man. But this being posited, the measurements and the shape of the cathedral were found to be such that it is exactly measured by musical lines which, emanating from a given point, reach one or another place in the cathedral and, instead of breaking down, reach it when they achieve their plenitude and fulfilment.

We can see in these examples that mathematics, music, architecture and all the additional elements which architecture brings into it – not only the shaping of space but also the conditioning of the echoes, the distances and so on – are of the same quality: they express a truth about relations. One of the elements of beauty is that it establishes relations and relationships.

May I interject at this point that, when we speak of aesthetics we speak not only of perception in general, but of a sensitive perception. The word 'aesthetics', which I cannot translate more precisely than 'perception' for lack of knowledge of English, could be connected in our minds with

[56]   Chartres Cathedral (Cathédrale Notre-Dame de Chartres): mostly constructed between 1194 and 1220, in a combination of the Romanesque and Gothic styles, it is designated a World Heritage Site by UNESCO, which calls it 'the high point of French Gothic art' and 'a masterpiece'.

the word 'anaesthetics': an anaesthetic is a drug that blots out not perception only but sensitivity in us. So when we think of aesthetics and in aesthetic terms, we relate to an object; when we remain indifferent to it, there is indeed no perception of beauty or ugliness; there is no perception at all of the object otherwise than something standing in our way which is irrelevant; and irrelevance is the contrary of all that life is made of, or aims at, or gives a meaning to. If all of us were totally irrelevant to one another, we would not perceive one another in any way except as a mass, an object, bulk, and this is what the aesthetic perception, the experience of beauty and ugliness prevents. So there is a very deep truth in the assertion that beauty is a convincing power of knowledge: not of intellectual knowledge, not of purely rational knowledge, but of a complex knowledge which implies intuition, reasoning, and which requires the participation of the total human being or the total society.

I think we must realise also that there are several elements that we are confronted with when we speak of beauty, as well as when we speak in scientific terms: there is reality, there is truth and there is us. Reality is more than truth. One can play on words (and both people who operate with Latin roots and people who operate with Slav roots have done it) and say that reality is what is and truth is what is and they both coincide! It is not quite like that. Thinking in scientific terms, let me say this: reality is both what we know and all that we do not know. No scientist would engage in research if he imagined that there was not in reality a whole wealth of the unknown. In that sense, a scientist approaches the world in the terms of the Epistle to the Hebrews, the eleventh chapter, where it says, 'Faith is certainty concerning things invisible.'[57] A scientist approaches the world, challenged by the visible, but his research goes into the invisible, or the yet unknown. Now, this is also very much the way in which we perceive beauty. We are challenged by a form, and beyond this form we may discover a content, a content that will be so meaningful, that it will light up the form and give it a meaning which the form itself does not possess. May I put it into one or two phrases? There is a spiritual writer called Methodius of Olympus,[58] who says:

> As long as we do not love a woman we are surrounded by women and by men; when we have given our heart to one woman, there is Her, with a capital H, and there are people.

In that short quotation, we see something very important: we were surrounded by an indiscriminate mass of people who were all significant up to a certain point, and irrelevant to a much greater extent. They were people; we had a contact with them from time to time, an exchange from time to time, and it ended at this; they dropped out of existence the

---

[57]   Hebrews 11:1.

[58]   St Methodius of Olympus (died *c.* 311), Church Father, bishop, ecclesiastical author and martyr, commemorated on 20 June.

moment they were out of sight. But then, one day, we look at a person and we suddenly see this person as we have never seen him or her before. It is as though we were looking at a drawing where everyone was drawn in pencil, that is in black or in grey, and, one day, someone had drawn one of these characters in red ink. It stands out, it is unique; all the rest is grey: there is only one person. This is commonplace in literature: to say that when someone is not there, everything has become empty.

But what is the process? What happens then? In some unaccountable way, by an act of intuition (that is of seeing, because *intuere* in Latin means 'see into'), we have seen something which we did not see before. But it is not the outer characteristics – we have seen these features, time and again. What we have not seen is the light shining through. We have seen a lamp that was not lit, then it was lit and it shone out with meaning, or simply with mystery: that is, with a challenge that said to us, 'There is in me something that you can discover, something unique, something ineffable, something with which (again, in the words of Lévy-Bruhl) you can enter into mystical participation; something that will be a relation in terms of communion, not simply of outer sharing but of an inter-wovenness that nothing can ever break afterwards.' There is a Russian saying: 'One meets a person once, but it is for ever, because having met, one cannot forget.' I am not speaking of our intellectual forgetfulness, but our whole self is marked and re-determined by this meeting. So, there is a reality that surrounds us, which is beyond the visible, beyond what we perceive, but which is the object of our search.

One may say that every one of us contains a chaos. Nietzsche[59] said somewhere, 'You must carry a chaos within yourself in order to give birth to a star.'[60] I think it is immensely important for us to realise the existence of this chaos and the importance of it.

When we speak of chaos habitually, we simply think in terms of disorder: 'My room is a chaos' means 'Do not come in because all the furniture is covered with books, linen and what not.' But it is not that. Chaos – if you look at it for instance in the beginning of the Bible – chaos is a state which is full of possibilities that have not yet found expression for themselves. It is pregnant with possibilities: all that is needed is to do something about them. What we usually tend to do is to try to put chaos into order in the same way in which we put in order our drawers, or our room and, therefore, kill any possibility for the chaos to give birth to a star!

[59] See footnote 17, Lecture 1.

[60] Friedrich Nietzsche, Prologue to *Thus Spake Zarathustra: A Book for All and None* (Also *Sprach Zarathustra: Ein Buch für Alle und Keinen*): philosophical novel containing ideas such as the 'eternal recurrence of the same', the parable on the 'death of God', and the 'prophecy' of the *Übermensch*; published in four parts 1883-1891.

LECTURE 2 – BEAUTY – PART 1

Those of you who read Bertolt Brecht[61] may have come upon a passage in which one of the characters says to another, 'Herr Keuner, when you are concerned with someone, when you love someone, what do you do about him?' and the answer is: 'I observe and study him.'

'And then what do you do?'

'I work out a blueprint of what is good for him.'

And then the interlocutor adds a damning phrase, a most unkind and unwanted phrase: the interlocutor says, 'Pray, which should comply with the other: the person or the blueprint?' and Herr Keuner answers, 'Of course, the person!'[62]

Well, this is exactly the way in which we deal with a chaos: that is, with all the possibilities pregnant within a situation, or within a person, which are frightening to us because we never know what will happen; and, therefore, to freeze it down, or to organise it *is* the simplest way. This is what is done by all the political and non–political systems: try to organise society, or an individual, so that there is absolutely no risk that something should emerge which is unforeseen and, therefore, will explode the ideal model which *I* have worked out, invented, and which *I*, therefore, cherish.

---

[61]   Eugen Berthold Friedrich 'Bertolt' Brecht (1898–1956), German theatre director, playwright, and poet.

[62]   Bertolt Brecht, *Stories of Mr Keuner* (*Geschichten vom Herrn Keuner*): appeared in various publications 1926-1956; first collection published posthumously, 1959.

There is another way, however, of looking at chaos. God deals with chaos quite differently. God calls out of the chaos all that is already mature and capable of emerging into life, or those things which are capable of emerging and of changing somehow into maturity. God does not aim at creating an order, He aims at creating a cosmos. I am sure all ladies will support my etymology if I remind you that the words 'cosmos' and 'cosmetics' are of the same root. It means 'creating beauty.'[63] When a lady uses war-paint, or other devices, to make her face into something which she finds is particularly beautiful and attractive, she is trying to do something which belongs to the process of creation. And that is what we are about concerning the cosmos: to call out of it a harmony, to call out of it a beauty which we cannot foresee; not a beauty according to our own taste, not a beauty according to our own presuppositions, but a beauty which will be a revelation to us of what are the potentialities of this cosmos.

Then, in the process we have got to speak of reality one way or another; we have got to find ways of expressing this cosmos in all its ambiguity between good and evil, between light and darkness, between life and death, between God and the adversary, between beauty and ugliness. But we can never do it adequately. When the ancient writers spoke of truth being the adequacy between reality and the mind, they did something very dangerous, because the great danger which

---

[63] Greek: κόσμος, order, ornament, world, universe.

is ours is to project the categories of our mind upon a reality which is much more complex, much richer, much greater and very much unknown to us. So the adequacy which we must aim at is not adequacy between the object which we contemplate and our mind, but adequacy between what we have seen of an object and the way in which we can express our experience of it; and that is quite a different thing. It may be a static expression. A snapshot, say, is very typically the immediate fixation of an object as it is now, at this moment, and it is perfectly true; there was a moment when you saw the object as it is in the photograph.

So often you see in a newspaper someone whose face could be very beautiful, but photographed from below with the mouth wide open, so that nothing is left but a big mouth and a ridiculous face. I remember a friend of mine presented me with a portrait of myself in the form of a sculpture. It was an oval, with metal strings and when I asked what it was, he said, 'I always think of you as someone who speaks,' and there was nothing but this horrible thing in which I refused to recognise my whole self! The point of what I am saying is not to try to convince you that I am not merely a mouth that speaks, but the fact that the moment you freeze down anything concerning life, it becomes a lie; it is no longer true; it is a betrayal. But then how can one describe things in a dynamic way? I will give you two examples:

The question is: 'What is it that I want to convey? Is it

to show the truth of the dynamic motion, or is it to fix the elements of it?' A first example:

The French sculptor, Rodin,[64] made a sculpture called *The Walking Man*,[65] and you see a man walking. Now, if you look at *The Walking Man*, you see that no man has ever walked that way, because Rodin's sculpture, being so big and so heavy, could never have stood on the ball of one foot, while the other was not on the ground. So the two feet are very solidly planted, because planted only on the toes of one foot it would not hold. But what he meant to do was not to show how a man actually walks, but the walk of the man, a walking man.

The same applies to a picture by the French painter, Géricault,[66] *The Derby at Epsom*.[67] You see that the horses are galloping. However, if you compare it to a snapshot you discover that not one horse gallops that way. The only thing is that on the snapshot you see horses that are suspended and petrified and do not budge at all: in the painting you see their gallop. And so, when we speak of the truth and try to

[64] François Auguste René Rodin (1840–1917), known as Auguste Rodin, French sculptor.

[65] Auguste Rodin, bronze sculpture, *L'homme qui marche* (1878).

[66] Jean-Louis André Théodore Géricault (1791–1824), French painter and lithographer, one of the pioneers of the Romantic movement in painting.

[67] Théodore Géricault, *Course de Chevaux*, traditionally called *Le Derby de 1821 à Epsom* (1821), in the Musée du Louvre.

convey it, we must be careful not to imagine that a static representation is truer than (all right) a falsified representation, but which conveys another element in it.

I was told yesterday that apart from every other shortcoming in my talk there was one very important one: that I had spoken for far too long. So I will stop here and leave the rest for my remaining two talks. If you feel like asking questions, or attacking me on what I have said, I am open and ready to answer if I can, and to be taught what I do not know, which is immense in this field.

QUESTIONS

I was wondering what you might say about envy of another's beauty. You seemed to want to say that love is the medium that enables us to see. Certainly, I have seen it happen: a case of envious perception of beauty; now, does that mean that in some sense this is not a true perception of beauty, or are we talking about a different kind of beauty?

When we see someone else's beauty, we can respond in two opposite ways: by envying it, or by marvelling at it, staying arrested by it with a sense of gratitude for what we are shown.

As far as envy is concerned, envy is a very curious feeling, because on the one hand, obviously, it is an attitude of mind which is far from being detached. It is not contemplative: we are wounded by someone's beauty because, at the moment of seeing the beauty, we compare with ourselves. It is a return to self. On the other hand, there is in envy a very important element: that we always envy one characteristic or another which we feel we lack, but we would never accept to change places with the other person. We might say, 'I would love to have your beautiful face, but not your husband;' 'I would like to have your physical beauty – you are a real Apollo – but not the job you have.'

So, in envy there is a very cruel attitude, which would deprive the other person of what is perhaps the most tender and precious gift of providence, and leave the other person with all that is hard, difficult, ugly in one way or another. I think there must be a whole education of self – not of others (Others we educate very easily!) but of self – in facing the good circumstances in which another person lives, the good, happy relationships or the beauty of a person, in an attitude of joy, of marvel.

In my final talk, I want to discuss an interview which the French singer, Jacques Brel,[68] once gave. He was ugly, and a rather determined interviewer had a long discussion with him on the way in which he dealt with his ugliness. I do not want to do it now, because I have enough difficulties in giving these talks without using up my material prematurely!

Our attitude to beauty is very ambiguous. When you were

[68]   Jacques Romain Georges Brel (1929–1978), Belgian singer, songwriter, actor and director, who lived, worked and died in France.

speaking of envy, I was thinking of other reactions to beauty. There is in the lives of saints a story about a spiritual guide, taking a stroll with his disciples and, as he was coming out of the city, there came towards them the most beautiful harlot, a common prostitute but of great beauty. The disciples covered their heads with their cloaks not to fall into temptation. But they fell into another temptation: they covered their faces so as not to see the girl, but they kept a loophole to see their master, to find out what he would do when confronted with this prostitute. And they saw him looking at her with an expression of contemplative ecstasy. When the woman had passed, and they felt safe, they said to him, 'How could you look at this woman; she is a prostitute!' And he answered, 'I did not see a prostitute; I saw the incredible beauty which God has given this woman.'[69]

You know, this kind of freedom from bringing things to self – 'Oh, the danger for me!' 'Oh, could I possess this characteristic or another!' – is something for which we must fight on moral grounds. I will come to that next time because I feel that, in all that we have got to say about beauty and the way in which we face it, there is a moral component and not only a psychological or a metaphysical one. There is beauty,

[69] See Benedicta Ward, *Harlots of the Desert: A Study of Repentance in Early Monastic Sources*, chapter 3, *Pelagia: Beauty Riding By* (1986). The story concerns St Pelagia of Antioch (also known as Pelagia the Harlot and Pelagia the Penitent), a Christian saint and hermit in the fourth or fifth century, commemorated 8 October. The spiritual guide is St Nonnus, bishop of Antioch, commemorated 2 December.

which is an absolute, and then there is the way in which we make it into something evil, because evil is in us, and not in it.

ॐ

I would like to expand that thought, because it does sometimes seem to me that something of this kind is at the root of racial or cultural friction. If we see something which we do not understand, which we cannot form into a pattern, we become actually hostile to it. I am thinking of the numerous English people, I am sure, who find this with Chinese script, and see it as sinister and somehow evil. It is a great discovery to find that there is a whole wealth of beauty in it. But the immediate reaction is to throw a brick at it! I think that is, to some extent, a cause of anti-Semitism. Jewish family life is different to Christian family life; therefore, it must be wrong in some way; and there is a reaction against it, an actual reaction of hatred against something which is beautiful.

Yes. I think it could not be more true. I have been a foreigner since the age of eight, in a variety of countries and situations. I know that, if you are a foreigner, you are really either an object of curiosity (exactly in the same way in which a monkey is, or another animal), or an object of rejection (if your ways or your attitudes do not fit), or an object of amusement.

When I came to this country a little more than thirty years ago and began to lecture on Orthodoxy, or to speak in

LECTURE 2 – BEAUTY – PART 1

public, my mother[70] said to me, 'I thought you wanted to be a priest, and I see that you have become a travelling circus!'

It was true, because – I dare say perhaps not in a University where you are more blasé about things, but in many places – people would come to listen to me just because I look odd: I wear sleeves such as no one else has. One can always hope that, being a foreigner, I would say something which is so inappropriate in English that everyone will be able to enjoy laughing at it!

I think it comes from the fact that – yes, indeed – we react negatively to what is alien to us. But I think before this, just a step before, there is always, or so often, a fear that something which is not within the compass of my experience, or the collective experience of the group to which I belong, may destroy or explode something which is precious to me or something which is my security. To discover that someone can think differently, before I can make a synthesis, or make a choice, may well be a frightening experience. That happens in scientific research. (I studied science and medicine; therefore, my mind works that way.) When you do scientific research, and have collected facts that are proven and solid, in order to keep them together and also to be able to use the whole of them, you build a model. But then, however honest you are, however much you want to reach out from your experience

[70] Metropolitan Anthony's mother, Xenia Nikolayevna Bloom, née Scriabina (1889-1958), was half-sister of the Russian composer and pianist, Alexander N. Scriabin.

73

into an objective reality which is beyond it, it is very difficult not to think, 'I hope that no one will find a fact that will contradict the facts that I have put together, or a flaw in the way in which I have put them together.' You find this, I am sorry to say, in all walks of life: people defending their conceptions, their theories, their religion, their philosophies, their politics, whatever, on the very limit of integrity, because it is so frightening to be left within an exploded world when you have been proved to be wrong.

So perhaps it is not primarily the strangeness of the other, but the fact that I am afraid that if what the other one is, or stands for, has enough substance, enough reality, enough truth in it, what will happen to my substance, my truth and my reality? Very often people project doubt, and their fear of doubt, from their own constructions on to the object. People are afraid of facing an argument against their view of God, of men, of the universe, of science. They are afraid of being challenged because they are afraid that if my view crumbles, where will my God be? Where will my most dear and precious experiences be? But in truth there is nothing to fear. These things will not be lost, because – as I tried to indicate in passing – unless we identify reality with our own projection, intellectual, rational projection, we risk nothing. Matter risks nothing from theories about it; neither does God risk anything from the variety of approaches to him. We may be the losers or the gainers, but there is nothing to fear in it.

LECTURE 2 – BEAUTY – PART 1

ॐ

Can you say something about the connection of Christian faith with the understanding of beauty, or perception of beauty?

If I may, I will quote Dostoyevsky,[71] who said that ultimately beauty is God in Christ.

From a human point of view, for a Christian, Christ is the fulfilment of human beauty and the revelation of divine beauty poured into Him. On another level, Christianity requires integrity of mind and heart, requires a moral attitude – not in terms of precepts to be kept, but of an approach which would rule out what the French writer, Malraux,[72] calls 'anti-arts', or 'anti-beauty', things which are morally destructive; because beauty should be more than an alluring or attractive form. To go far back beyond Malraux, I would say that the Greek definition of a complete man as καλὸς κἀγαθός,[73] the man who is beautiful, good and brave, could be a formula which approaches the

---

[71] See footnote 24, Lecture 1.

[72] André Malraux (1901–1976), French novelist, hero of the French resistance, and later art theorist and Minister of Cultural Affairs under President de Gaulle. In addition to the Légion d'honneur and other honours, he was awarded the Distinguished Service Order by the United Kingdom for his work with British liaison officers in occupied France during World War II.

[73] Καλὸς κἀγαθός (kalos kagathos), Greek: beautiful and well-born, brave, good; a phrase used by classical Greek writers to describe an ideal of gentlemanly personal conduct, especially in a military context.

Christian way of thinking. I think that a Christian would rule out morally destructive forms because they may be a lie against a deeper and truer reality.

I think I have been so confused that I would not be surprised if you have understood nothing of my answer! I will try to be more intelligible tomorrow!

Lecture 3 – Beauty – Part 2

3 November 1982

I must first say something which belongs still to yesterday's subject, and then move on to what is really the subject of this evening, to bridge the gap between my first lecture on beauty, and what I have to say about the meaning of ugliness which, I believe, is an important thing for us to assess and understand

I said yesterday that one of the definitions which were given of truth was: equivalence between the object and the intellect, and that I found this kind of definition dangerous, because the equivalence is not between the intellect and the object, since the intellect has its own categories. Rather it is between the mysterious, complex reality which we perceive only partly, which we assess imperfectly, and the expression which one can give to it – and that in a very relative manner, in proportion to the perception and in proportion to our ability to express what we have perceived. But when it comes to expressing things, as I mentioned yesterday, there are two quite different approaches. The one is an attempt at simple verisimilitude, trying to create an image which is as resemblant to the object as possible, but even here there are difficulties because: what is true verisimilitude? What is really the image of the object which we see? Speaking in terms of comparison, is it a snapshot, or is it a portrait? A snapshot gives an exact image of a face, or a situation, or a scene, at a given moment. But is it true? Well, in a way it is not true at all, because it is a face, or a scene taken out of the flow of life: this face does not look like this all the time. On the other hand, a portrait does not attempt simply to reproduce features of a given moment.

I would like to read you a quotation which I found by chance (and I rejoice at the chance which gave it to me), by a man called Robert Heinlein.[74] He says:

> *An artist can look at a pretty girl and see the old woman she will become. A better artist can look at an old woman and see the pretty girl she used to be. A great artist can look at an old woman, portray her exactly as she is and force the viewer to see the pretty girl she used to be. More than that, he can make anyone, even with the sensibility of an armadillo, see that this lovely girl is still alive — prisoned inside her ruined body. He can make you feel the quiet, endless tragedy that there was earlier a girl born who never grew older than eighteen in her heart, no matter what the merciless hours have done.*[75]

---

[74]   Robert Anson Heinlein (1907-1988), American science fiction writer. His sometimes controversial works continue to influence the genre of science fiction, and modern culture more generally.

[75]   Robert Heinlein, novel, *Stranger in a Strange Land* (1961).

LECTURE 3 – BEAUTY – PART 2

This is also verisimilitude, but of another type. It is a vision that allows one to look at the moment and see all that the past has brought to this moment. Because every moment of ours is a summing up, or the sum total rather, of all our past, but we do not discern it: usually we see only what appears on the surface, brought forth by circumstances and time.

So, verisimilitude is important, but which one? Is it that of the portrait, is it that of the snapshot, or is it perhaps a vision even greater: a vision that does away practically with material evidence and with mere appearances? If I may I will give you an image taken from the Gospels, although I have tried to avoid being clerical and speaking in terms of the Holy Scripture. It is the story of Christ and the woman taken in adultery. She is brought to Him, she is accused, she is condemned by the law of the Old Testament and by the attitude of the Jews that bring her. Christ is asked what his judgement would be. His answer is, 'Let him who is without sin cast the first stone.' And then, when everyone has gone, he asks her, 'Where are those who have condemned you? They have gone. Neither do I condemn you; go in peace, but sin no more.'[76]

Now, the way in which I read the story is really the point which I am making. It was not appearances He was brushing away, it was not a false accusation like that which brought

[76] John 8:2-11.

81

to trial Susannah in the Old Testament, falsely accused;[77] it was material evidence, it was factual evidence. But what did he do about it? Does it mean that he simply rejected the evidence, considered that there was no reason for it? No. What he saw was the law, and beyond the material evidence something else: here was a girl who had sinned grievously; here was a girl who, if she remained what she was, an adulteress, deserved condemnation; but what he saw is that this girl had foolishly committed adultery, because she had never become aware of an essential fact of life: that sin (evil) and death (destruction) belong together, that sin contains in itself death and destruction. And here she was brought unto judgement knowing that the result of it would be her death. And, confronted with death, she had seen herself in a different way. Christ was not letting go an adulteress because He was kind-hearted, or because He was easy-going, or because he might have approved of a permissive society: He let go a girl who was confronted with death and had discovered that evil, sin, was co-extensive with dying, and who could go back into life having gone through the gates of death and understood what she had never known before. So, in a way, there is also this element in our vision of things: the ability to see in depth

---

[77]   The story of *Susannah and the Elders*, recounted in chapter 13 of the *Book of Daniel* in the *Septuagint*. Two elders spy on the beautiful Susannah as she bathes, then try to blackmail her into having sexual relations with them. When she refuses, they accuse her of promiscuity and she is tried, but Daniel intervenes and demands the elders be questioned. Thus they are found to have accused her falsely, and are put to death.

not what there is not, but what there truly is, beyond what could be an object of verisimilitude, that is of copying the form without perceiving the deepest content.

Now, speaking of the real, I mentioned the fact that the visible may be unreal, untrue. It may appear as an illusion, as a distortion; it may appear as a surface without any depth; it may be an imperfect expression of something real and true; it may be a form that is a lie and a lure. Speaking of the visible world in terms of unreality, one could mention the Indian attitude to the existing world as *maya*,[78] as an illusion. It is there, but it is deeply unreal and untrue somehow.

It may also be that the visible is simultaneously a veil and a revelation. A veil because reality is deeper, greater, more significant, more meaningful than the forms which we can apprehend, but it is also the only means we possess to cross through the forms which we can apprehend to perceive a reality, a meaning which is within them. I have no time to make quotations, but there are a number of writings on the pantheistic side, beginning with antiquity and going through up to our time. I am thinking at the moment particularly of a French writer, Gérard de Nerval,[79] who looks at reality and says:

[78] Sanskrit – *maya*, literally 'illusion' or 'magic', has multiple meanings in Indian philosophies. As a spiritual concept it connotes 'that which exists but is constantly changing and thus is spiritually unreal', and the 'power or the principle that conceals the true character of spiritual reality'.

[79] Gérard de Nerval, nom–de–plume of the French writer, poet, essayist and translator, Gérard Labrunie (1808-1855).

Beware: within the visible reality that seems to be inert, that seems not to be alive with all the intensity which we see in the word 'life', there is a life hidden.[80]

An ancient writer said, 'Cleave a stone and you will see there is life within it.'[81] And others have said things of the same kind. One could quote a writer like Vladimir Solovyov,[82] in the Russian tradition, who says, 'My friend, do you not understand that all that you hear is the echo of a music which is beyond us?'[83]

I have spoken of chaos yesterday and of the fact that both within us, in our midst, and in the total universe we are confronted with chaos, not in the sense of mere disorder, a disorder resulting from the collapse of order, but of a mysterious reality, pregnant with possibilities, which are not yet expressed and which are waiting for the moment when they will be mature to flower, to blossom out, and to appear in glory

Now, there is a problem of expression, static and

[80]   *Gérard de Nerval, The Daughters of Fire (Les Filles du feu*, 1854), collection of short prose works, poetry and a play.

[81]   Cf the apocryphal *Gospel of Thomas*, discovered near Nag Hammadi, Egypt, in December 1945: 'Jesus says, "… Cleave the wood: I am there; lift the stone and thou shalt find me there!"'

[82]   Vladimir Sergeyevich Solovyov (1853-1900), Russian philosopher, theologian, poet, pamphleteer, and literary critic.

[83]   Vladimir S. Solovyov, poem, 'My friend, do you not understand' (*Милый друг, иль ты не видишь*, 1892).

dynamic, and there are a variety of ways in which this expression is attempted. If we belong to a certain cultural background, a certain cultural tradition, allusions may convey expression to us in the form of reminiscences, awakening in us our own experience already perceived in past understanding. You can find that time and again in T. S. Eliot; you can find that in so many authors, both poets and not, in whom we can hear the echoes of things that have been said or written in the past, and so which enrich every word and every image given. There are also allegories and myths, which are liable at times and within limits to more than one interpretation, but which, like so many images, are meant to have more than one interpretation because the person who presents them presents either one facet which he has perceived and expressed in these terms, or presents an image which is more convincing to him than anything he could say, because he is aware that whatever he will say will be limiting his experience, while the image conveys it more than words could do, or any statement could do.

In this line, one can speak of the analogy and similitude which one can find by drawing parallels. The French writer, Paul Valéry,[84] translates, in an imagery which is totally different from what he speaks about, his vision of what he sees: indeed, at times you need a commentary that explains every image and every line, because it is anything but obvious. But then,

---

[84] Ambroise Paul Toussaint Jules Valéry (1871-1945), French poet, essayist and philosopher.

perhaps, a saying of Stéphane Mallarmé,[85] another French poet, explains it. He was a teacher in the secondary school which I attended – a number of years, of course before I was there, but there were still echoes of his presence. I remember an old man, who had been a pupil in his time, reporting that one of the other teachers said to him, 'Monsieur Mallarmé, I cannot understand your poetry.' And Mallarmé looked at him and said, 'I am not surprised, Sir, I write only for intelligent people.'

And then there are attempts to convey the glimpse of reality perceived – that is the experience of reality – in symbolic ways. A symbol in ancient Greece was something very simple: when two friends parted and one of them was to go far away and thought he might send a message that was to be received with certainty, without doubt, they took either a coin, or a piece of pottery and broke it. The messenger was to bring the half, and if the half fitted exactly then the messenger was a true messenger and the message was reliable.[86] In that sense, every symbolic expression is half of a broken coin, and can be recognised only if we possess the other half of it. That means that it requires human, cultural experience or, at times,

---

[85] Stéphane (Étienne) Mallarmé (1842–1898), French symbolist poet and critic.

[86] Greek: σύμβολον, tally, i.e. each of two halves of an ἀστράγαλος or other object, which two contracting parties, broke between them, each party keeping one piece, in order to have proof of the identity of the presenter of the other; guarantee, token, passport, treaty, contract, receipt, warrant, omen, symptom, watchword, religious creed.

transcendental experience like the writings of the mystics. Examples could be so many. There is a German poet called Scheffel,[87] who has written a song, a love song, about his parting from his beloved, and he draws a continuous parallel between the landscape, the weather, the greyness of the day, and the sorrow that is within his heart.[88] This is a simple kind of symbol: the world is grey, the wind is blowing and whistling through the fronds of the trees, the rain is falling hard – truly the right weather to say good-bye! – and so he goes on. This is half of the broken coin: we all possess the other half. At times the imagery is more complex, and I dare say that it may be so complex, or so momentarily true, that even the author may stumble when you ask him what he meant. There is a letter of the Russian poet, Blok,[89] who is one of the greatest of the symbolist poets, in which he says:

> *When I re-read my poetry that was so clear to me, in which all the symbols were so evident, some of them I cannot understand any more. They corresponded to a moment's vision, and they have gone.*[90]

---

[87] Joseph Victor von Scheffel (1826–1886), German poet and novelist.

[88] Joseph Victor von Scheffel: Young Werner's Songs XII, from the epic poem, *The Trumpeter of Säkkingen* (*Der Trompeter von Säkkingen*, 1854).

[89] Alexander Alexandrovich Blok, (1880–1921), Russian lyrical poet.

[90] This is an approximate translation of Blok's letter, perhaps made by Metropolitan Anthony from memory.

So, when *we* read it, we may see something else, or we may see nothing, or we may recapture his experience which he had lost.

There is also a way of conveying things which I do not understand in terms of poetry or prose, but which I think I understand a little bit more, if not to excess, in abstract art. Apart from the attempts by some abstract painters to be simply doing something unheard of – and that exists in all walks of life – there are some who feel that one must break the models, the models being the intellectual categories which have been projected, century after century, on the objects, or the situations, or the experiences which surround us. They believe that experience of the visible, or audible or perceptible world has been made a prisoner of intellectual categories and they must be broken, as a model is broken, so that one can breathe. And so that one can, having got rid of a superimposed, rational structure, achieve something else: a new vision. I will give you an example, or an image, which really is on the fringe of what I am saying.

There is a book by a man called Gregory,[91] who is Professor of Psychology at Bristol, which is called *The Intelligent Eye*,[92] and he shows in his book how often we recognise things, we see things, because we know how to look at them and how to discern them. And he shows a very

---

[91] Richard Langton Gregory, CBE, FRS, FRSE (1923-2010), Emeritus Professor of Neuropsychology at the University of Bristol, who worked especially in the field of cognitive psychology.

[92] Richard Gregory, *The Intelligent Eye* (1970)

interesting photograph. He has a photograph in which there is a Dalmatian dog (you know, one of those big dogs who seem to have measles – covered with spots) standing against the background of a piece of land covered with puddles. The puddles and the spots of the dog are more or less of the same size. Now, obviously, when we see a dog usually, we see him in relief, in motion and so on. But when we see a dog standing against this background, the dog is normally marked by a line that delimits him. Here Gregory has done away with the line, and you cannot see the dog! You do not see the dog until, after great efforts, you have singled out two smaller puddles, which are his eyes, two more small puddles, which are his nostrils, then you are surprised that there is an oblong puddle and you realise, 'Oh, that is the shadow of its tail,' and, gradually, you can reconstruct the dog! I feel that at times abstract art is aiming at this dislocation of a conventional view, of a view on which we have forced our intellectual schemes and forms, in order to look anew. Obviously, when you look at a Dalmatian dog against that background it is in the end a Dalmatian dog you will see but, in other realms, the fact of dislocating this kind of reality, looking at it again may allow you, help you, see things with quite new eyes. There is newness in the vision, which you could not obtain by looking again and again while you project your categories.

The French writer, Malraux,[93] has said that the

---

[93] See footnote 72, Lecture 2.

contemplation of the surrounding world, together with the perception of beauty and ugliness – the artistic vision and not simply the practical, the utilitarian vision of the surrounding world – must lead us to vision first, then to reflection: not to a sort of post-mortem of what we have seen, but to a deeper reflection of what it means to us, or what it may mean in itself, and then to a sort of exorcising of what we are presented with from our intellectual categories, a liberation of ourselves from the imprisonment in our human structures, an effort to learn to see an object and not to see ourselves, or our pre-conceived interpretation. Of course, there is a danger of projecting these human categories, but still, we can try and learn. We can do this (and I have already spoken of this, so I am not going to repeat it) – we can do this if we learn to look at things in a selfless, in a detached, in a serene way; selfless in the sense that we must not look at things and ask ourselves, 'How does it affect me?' I must see the thing, and not myself, either projected, or reflected, or endangered, or gratified by what I see, and with a serenity which is born from this very freedom from the fear or the greed attaching to our usual approach to whatever, or even whoever, surrounds us.

And then, in the end, there is the very complex world of the parables. Far too often we think of parables as visual aids, in the same way in which, in a comic, one has an illustration that conveys nothing more than what the text provides, but which adds to some sort of dramatic perception of it. But a parable is something a great deal richer and more interesting,

Lecture 3 – Beauty – Part 2

because it involves the object – and that is ourselves – and it involves all our capabilities of imagination and of experience in an almost endless way. May I just dwell on that for a few moments, and dwell in terms of geometric figures?

You know that a circle has got a centre. Now a statement which is complete in itself, which is self-explanatory, is like a circle with a centre. You can go to the centre and you possess all the figure. A factual statement of any kind will correspond to this kind of image. An ellipse is an oblong figure which really is like a circle on which someone is sitting and has squashed it in height; it possesses two half-circles which are incomplete, linked with two curves but, at the centre of each of these curves there is a focal point, and these two focal points have a very curious correspondence between themselves. When you are truly possessed of what there is in one of the focal points, you can perceive what is in the other one, and vice versa. This is the principle of the whispering galleries in architecture. If you stand at the focus of one end of the ellipse, and someone stands at the other focus, a very quiet whispering is heard absolutely clearly, while the voice is perceived nowhere else within the limits of the ellipse.

Well, that is a very important way of conveying things in words, in music, in all forms of expression. The creator speaks at one point but, in order to hear him, you cannot go to the point where he is, because you cannot simply identify with him to the point of sharing his experience in the way in which he perceives it. Instead you can go to the other focus and hear exactly what he says. And I think this is one of the ways in which a poet speaks of his experience, and calls out, brings out, conjures out your own, by sharing with you his to such an extent, in such a way that you become the richer for it. You share, yes, but it is not an invented, or borrowed experience, it is an experience which is called out of you in the way in which, image for image, the whole world, in the first chapter of the Bible, is called out of chaos by a creative word that says to everything that can be, 'Come!' and it comes, revealing itself and being a revelation at the same time.

And then there is a very curious figure in mathematics called a parabola. A parabola (I am sorry, I am not a mathematician, and probably not all of you are, but, speaking again in images) – a parabola is something like an ellipse which has lost half of its existence. That is: there is a beginning of a half-circle, and then the two arms, that in an ellipse would meet the other half-circle, simply open out. Now, a parabola possesses a centre, a focus, but if you take the summit of this parabola and go through the focus, there is a line that goes into infinity. And that is the point, I think, in which a real parable is so interesting, because you can take hold of this centre which is there before your eyes, before your nose, which is accessible, and then from there look into infinity and go along this line as far as you will be able to go. You – not another person! I may go an inch; you may go a yard; someone else will go a mile, but it will be along this line, and it is possible because you have begun at this end, at the point at which someone has said, 'Here it is. Start!'

This is what we can find in the more complex parables of the Gospels, and in so many parables of east and west. The parable of whatsoever tradition or culture is built on that very principle: a focal point which is within your perception, but does not call you to stay at this point; on the contrary, tells you, 'Go away into infinity, as long and as far as you can go!'

What is curious with art is that an expression that is a form, whether it is oral, vocal, whether in words or sound or shape, is something which is born from an experience and is the embodiment of a content: a content which is mediated by the artist, a content which he has perceived and projected in his piece of art. But then this form to him, and to the people who belong together with him in culture, or in spiritual, or intellectual or emotional experience, conveys something of his own knowledge: knowledge not only rational and intellectual, but total.

But then centuries go by, and what happens is that the form remains. We possess pieces of art created hundreds and thousands of years ago. We cannot always recapture the intention of the person who created it: for instance, when it is born from a religious tradition which has died out and to which we have no access, or about which we can have our guesses but in which we do not participate; or when it is taken from a cultural tradition to which we have no access because it is so profoundly different that we do not know how to coincide with the experience. Then we are confronted with a form that claims from us a response, and this response will be at times a new content, not totally different from the one which was the cause, the original cause of this piece of art, but a new content which will be born of the little we know, the little we can perceive and the amount which we possess within ourselves. In that case, there is a pouring into an existing form of something which perhaps was not there originally, or else was there as part of the universal human experience, but not the particular experience in time, space and history. I have little to say about this, but I saw by accident a performance on television of *Don Quixote*[94] this winter. (I happened to be in front of a television which I normally never see.) You remember that the story of Don Quixote ends with his discovering his folly, and his return to sanity. Now the whole story of Don Quixote was presented in this television programme adequately, obviously in an abbreviated way, as Cervantes[95] has presented it, but it was reversed: he comes to his senses, but then the whole vision crumbles and he is brought back to believing that his previous vision of the world was truer than what the sane person sees of

[94]   *The Ingenious Nobleman Sir Quixote of La Mancha (El Ingenioso Hidalgo Don Quijote de la Mancha)*, or simply *Don Quixote*, Spanish novel by Miguel de Cervantes, published in two parts in 1605 and 1615, *Don Quixote* is the most influential work of literature from the Spanish Golden Age and the entire Spanish literary canon. It has been translated into over 140 languages and dialects, and is, after the Bible, the most-translated book in the world.

[95]   Miguel de Cervantes Saavedra (1547?-1616 (NS)), Spanish writer widely regarded as the greatest writer in the Spanish language and one of the world's pre-eminent novelists.

it. This conveyed a new message out of an old form. Obviously, it was unfaithful to Cervantes, it was untrue to his intention but, in a way, it was legitimate as far as the new perception was concerned.

Now, to establish a bridge between what I have said so far and what I still intend to say in our next talk to the survivors of this series, I would like to say that I have been speaking all this time of beauty in purely human terms: that is in terms of physical and psychological realities. But within the Christian tradition, and outside of it, there is a very strong sense that beauty, the notion of beauty, applies also to spiritual achievement. The early writers of Christianity, of the undivided Christian world (so one can speak of it without any nuances) said that to become truly a person is to create a piece of art. St Irenaeus of Lyon,[96] in the second century, said that:

A man perfectly fulfilled is the splendour of God.[97]

In the Orthodox tradition the spiritual struggle is expressed in terms of achieving supreme beauty. The books which contain

[96]   St Irenaeus of Lyon (*c.*130–*c.*202), Bishop of Lugdunum (now Lyon), originally from Smyrna, noted for guiding and expanding Christian communities in what is now the south of France, and for the development of Christian theology by combatting heresy and defining orthodoxy. His best-known work is *On the Detection and Overthrow of the So-Called Gnosis*, often cited as *Adversus Haereses, an attack on Gnosticism.*

[97]   Latin, *Gloria enim Dei vivens homo*, from St Irenaeus of Lyon, *Adversus Haereses,*

the ascetic and mystical teachings of Orthodoxy are grouped under the name of *Philokalia*,[98] which means 'the love of beauty', not of external beauty, but of a beauty that holds together the spiritual greatness of man, his psychological harmony and his bodily harmony. And I think this is a very important thing to remember: that beauty is something that is not only (speaking in creationist terms) – is not only something that applies to the created, but also to the uncreated, to the communion – what Lévy-Bruhl[99] calls the 'mystical participation' – of man not only in the objects of this world, but in the creator of this world. And when we find, for instance, in St Peter's Epistle General, the call that we should become 'partakers of the divine nature',[100] it is not only in terms of holiness, or harmony, of purity, of sanity in every respect that we can speak, but also in terms of supreme beauty: a vision of what is truth and beyond truth, a vision of what is reality, unveiling itself before us and which is the convincing power of this reality. A beauty which is indeed in the eye and heart of the beholder, because we must have eyes to see, but not only in a passive way, because participation, communion, entering

[98] The *Philokalia* (Greek: φιλοκαλία 'love of the beautiful, the good', from φιλία (*philia*) 'love' and κάλλος (*kallos*) 'beauty'), a collection of the writings of Eastern Orthodox hesychast spiritual masters of the fourth–fifteenth centuries, originally written for the instruction of monks in the practice of contemplation. Compiled in the eighteenth century by St Nicodemus the Hagiorite and St Macarius of Corinth.

[99] See footnote 49, Lecture 2.

[100] Peter 1:4.

into an experience requires from us the same kind of struggle, the same kind of intense, ruthless attitude to ourselves which a true artist applies to himself when he is confronted with a piece of granite or of marble or an empty canvas, and must look at this piece of granite and see within it the statue which he must free from its imprisonment in the stone. But that implies, yes, it does imply the existence also of what Malraux calls 'anti-arts': all the forms of creativeness indeed which instead of enhancing human reality, bring it down, prevent greatness, prevent our growth into a measure of beauty by replacing genuine beauty with a falsification of it.

I will end this talk by reading to you a passage from Dostoyevsky,[101] in which he opposes two kinds of beauty. Dostoyevsky had an idea – and you will probably have heard the phrase – that 'it is beauty that will save the world.'[102] Not everyone is capable of perceiving intellectual truth; not everyone is capable of perceiving many of the things which reach us through our reasoning powers. But there is no-one who is not capable of responding to whatever faces him in terms of beauty or ugliness.

I was amazed a couple of years ago, when I wanted to give a talk on beauty and thought that I would find it all ready-made in the *Encyclopaedia Britannica*, to discover that there is

[101]   See footnote 24, Lecture 1.

[102]   Fyodor M. Dostoyevsky, *The Idiot* (Идиот), published serially in the magazine, *The Russian Herald* (Русский вестник), in 1868-9.

no entry for 'Beauty' in it. But if you look up 'Aesthetics' you will find two lines saying, 'Beauty being a purely subjective experience, nothing can be said about it.'

The trouble is that it may be subjective as far as the choice is concerned of what I or you find beautiful, but it is a universal reaction, or response to everything whether it is a moral situation or whether it is an object. You can present an object to anyone and ask, 'What do you think of it?' and he would say, 'Oh, how ugly!' or 'How lovely!' and that is exactly where beauty or ugliness, which are correlative, come into the picture. So that Dostoyevsky's phrase 'Beauty will save the world', means that anyone is capable of responding to truth in terms of beauty, or rejecting ugliness because it is a lie against reality, or a distortion, or a calumny of it, or a lure. And then Dostoyevsky goes on to say that there are two kinds of beauty: there is the real beauty which elevates, and there is the beguiling beauty which belongs to human greed, to human meanness, to human sensuality detached from the deep and real feelings.

I will come to that in my last talk. I would like to end this one with this quotation (I am sorry for the translation. It's bad, although it is not mine!):

What is artistic reality? They say that artistic work must reflect life and so forth; all that is rubbish. The writer creates life, a life in such full amplitude as did not exist before him.

LECTURE 3 – BEAUTY – PART 2

That is one example of what he means, and then:

The need for beauty and the creation which embodies it is inseparable from man, and without it man would not want to live in the world. Man thirsts for it, finds and accepts beauty unconditionally and just because it is beauty, and he bows before it with reverence, without asking what it is useful for, or what one can buy for it. And perhaps precisely in this consists the greatest secret of art, that the image of beauty created by it immediately becomes an idol unconditionally.

And why does it become an idol? Because the need for beauty develops most at the moment man is in discord with reality, in disharmony, in struggle; that is, when he is living most of all, because man lives most of all when he is seeking something and striving. At such a time, he feels within himself a most natural desire for everything harmonious, for tranquillity, and in beauty there is both harmony and tranquillity.

But, when man finds what he has been striving for, then, for a time, life as it were, slows up for him, and we have seen examples in which man, having achieved the ideal of his desires, not knowing what farther to strive for, being satiated, would fall into a kind of anguish, would even foment in himself this anguish, seeking out another ideal in his life, and out of extreme surfeit of pleasure not only would not value what he had enjoyed, but consciously would even turn from the direct path, exciting in himself alien tastes – unhealthy, sharp, lacking in harmony – sometimes monstrous ones, losing measure and aesthetic feeling for healthy beauty and demanding instead of it exceptions. And therefore, beauty is immanent in everything healthy, that is in that which is most alive and is a necessity of the human being. It is harmony; in it lies the guarantee of tranquillity; it embodies the ideals of man and of mankind. [103]

I do not agree with every word which I have just read, but I wanted to confront you with this attitude of Dostoyevsky's, and with this view he has that there are two kinds of beauty, the one which is fulfilment and leads to plenitude, and the one which is what a French aestheticist[104] calls in French *art d'assoupissement*,[105] that is arts which are aimed at filling an emptiness, arts that are arts of consumption, not arts which are beauty in themselves, but which are devoured and used in order to fill an emptiness to satiate us because we are hungry and we are incapable of facing greatness and look for food at the lowest possible level.

This is the end of this talk of mine, and you will be glad to know that the next one will be the last!

[103]   Fyodor M. Dostoyevsky, article, 'Mr –bov and the Question of Art' (Г-н -бов и вопрос об искусстве), published in the magazine *Epoch* (Эпоха) in 1865.

[104]   Georges Albert Maurice Victor Bataille (1897-1962), French intellectual and literary figure working in literature, philosophy, anthropology, economics, sociology and history of art.

[105]   'The art of drowsiness' – from *assoupir*, to make drowsy, to dull the senses or passions.

QUESTIONS

You seem to think that it would be proper to approach our environment without structures, without any preconceptions, and without a scheme in which we are going to put phenomena with which we are daily confronted. On the other hand, you said that when we actually do confront the natural world we see in it beauty which is inherent in the natural world, and it would seem more reasonable to suggest that beauty was in fact a structure which we impose on the world, and likewise for ugliness, and that the very notion that we approach the world without structures was a little fanciful.

What I mean to say is that we approach most things with a preconceived idea and with a ready structure which we will impose upon it, instead of being, as it were, vacant, open and ready to meet whatever will come our way. In a second move of our heart, or mind or whatever, of our whole personality, we can assess what we have seen in certain terms, but we must begin with approaching whatever will come our way with openness and be able to see. I will give you two examples, one which is very trivial and very simple, and the other which, to me, is very moving.

If a boy or a girl at school is called to the headmaster or headmistress, what they expect is to meet the headmaster or the headmistress; they never expect to meet a person, and the whole orientation is to meet that function, but not that person. The same would be true … I remember when

101

I was a private in the beginning of the war and was called to see the sergeant major. I did not expect him to be anything else but the sergeant major, and it meant danger, dread and expectation of the worst! So this is a way in which, before we have even looked at an object, we know what to expect and, therefore, we do not see what there is there, because you may well discover that your sergeant major, or the headmaster or whomever you meet is quite a different person if you only look.

I want to make a parenthesis between that and the second example: I spoke once in Oxford, at the chaplaincy, to a group of students on 'Encounter' – on the conditions of a fruitful and intelligent encounter between people. The chaplain in those remote days said to me, 'Well, you are speaking of the impossible. You say that you must look at people and see them, listen to them and hear them; but I see so many people: I cannot possibly listen to and hear and see them all as you suggest; they speak to me and then they pass.' And I said, 'Well, you could perhaps begin with something less than all the floods of students who run through your room; you might begin with seeing or hearing one of the people closest to you.' He was a man in his fifties, and he said, 'Well, could you give me an example?' I said, 'Yes. Shut your eyes.' So he shut his eyes. I said, 'Would you tell me what is the colour of your wife's eyes?' He opened his eyes, looked at me – not at his wife! – and said sheepishly, 'I cannot remember.' The fact is that, when he was in love with her, he probably had eyes for nothing but her eyes; he looked into her eyes, he saw nothing but her eyes. But then they got married – they had been married thirty years – there was no longer any point in looking at one another! They walked shoulder to shoulder through life, and what was the point of all these things which one does at the beginning of life? He could not even say what her eyes were like! What can you expect after that?!

Now, the other example which I want to give is quite an earnest one.

An old Russian woman, who died a few years ago, who was the wife of Lewis Namier, the historian, [106] in the course of the Revolution, in the beginning, was arrested, put into prison and eventually spent a number of years in a concentration camp. She told me that, while she was in prison, she was being interrogated every night for hours and hours and hours, cross-examined, interrogated again, cross-examined again until exhaustion broke her completely. And one night, in the early hours of the morning, when all her

---

[106]   The 'old Russian woman' was Lady Julia Namier (1893-1977), *née* Iulia Michaelovna Kazarina, who wrote under the name, Iulia de Beausobre. Her first husband, Nicolai de Beausobre, a Russian diplomat, died in the communist persecution of the 1930s, and Iulia herself was committed to a prison camp. She was ransomed by her former governess, a British woman, and migrated to Britain in 1934. In Britain she wrote *The Woman Who Could Not Die* (autobiography, 1938) and *Creative Suffering* (1940). In 1947 she married the historian, Sir Lewis Namier. After his death in 1960, she wrote his biography.

.

energy had ebbed down, when there was no courage left in her, she felt she could not endure it any more, that even at the risk of being sent into a punishment cell, of enduring anything, she must break the spell of this endless, repetitive interrogation. So she looked up at her interrogator, ready to challenge him, to provoke him so that the spell be broken. And, she said to me, she looked at him and what she saw was a face grey with tiredness, with anguish in his eyes because he had spent exactly as many hours as she had at this interrogation; he was as exhausted and tired as she was. And, in a flash, she thought that there was no difference between them: only that the whirlwind of the Revolution had cast him, like a dry leaf, on one side of the table, and her on the other side, but they were prisoners of the same situation: that he too was a human being in agony. And, having seen that, she smiled at him. He smiled back and the interrogation continued, but the spell was broken; they had seen one another as human beings.

And that is what I mean: that instead of seeing in that man nothing but the interrogator, she saw a human being. And if we did that with regard to objects, animals, people, situations, we would be able to see in a way in which we do not see when we look at a thing with greed. You know, 'Live beef! Live beef!' when you see cattle, does not lend you any secret of what an animal is; and that is what I wanted to point out.

Now, in a second step, of course, you must reflect. We have an intelligence: it must be as acute, as precise, as sensitive as possible. We have perceptiveness and sensitivity, which must be used to the utmost. But to understand what is in front of us as truly as possible, by disengaging ourselves and not seeing things only in relation to us; then we could probably see more.

ॐ

Could I ask why you do not quote from English poets? Because all the time you have been saying, 'Truth is beauty,' I keep thinking of Keats.[107]

Well, the answer is sadly and infinitely simple: because of ignorance! You know, the trouble is that I came to this country when I was thirty-five years old and began to learn English just before I came, about three months before, using the *Authorized Version*,[108] so that when I came to this country all the knowledge of English I possessed was contained in the beginnings of *Genesis*, grammar and vocabulary inclusive, and you can imagine how it developed! I have tried to read as much as I could since, but I have difficulty in quoting English poets because they are less familiar to me. You know,

---

[107] John Keats (1795-1821), one of the main figures of the second generation of English Romantic poets, along with Lord Byron and Percy Bysshe Shelley. See also Lecture 4.

[108] The *Authorised Version*, or *King James Bible*: an English translation of the Bible made between 1604 and 1611 under the sponsorship of King James I, which became the standard translation used by the Church of England, and across the English-speaking world until the mid-twentieth century.

however much you have read in adult life, you probably read a great deal when you were at school and discovered things. I discovered children's books when I was in my forties, when my English had improved from *Genesis* to colloquial English. I have been trying to read more prose than poetry because, unfortunately, I am called to speak, and people do not expect me to speak in verse! And also, I have difficulties with a number of English poets because my knowledge of English is imperfect, and it takes me a very long time to find a way in which I can read an English poem so that it reaches me as a poem and not as a statement. So I do apologise. I am ashamed of myself, but the answer is ignorance.

In your comments about arts aimed at filling emptiness, what creates that emptiness?

My answer, but I speak in the first person, in 'I' terms, is what Michael Ramsay[109] said once, that within each human being there is an emptiness as vast as God, and it can be filled by nothing but Him. And I think that unless we grow in spirit, unless we develop not only all our physical qualities, not only all our psychological qualities (and I lump everything in that),

[109]   Arthur Michael Ramsey, Baron Ramsey of Canterbury, PC (1904–1988), 100th Archbishop of Canterbury, 1961-1974, previously Bishop of Durham and Archbishop of York. He was known as a theologian, educator, and advocate of Christian unity.

but also our spirit, there will be a sense of hunger, of needing something more, and then we will try to fill the space with a variety of things. Now, when you think of a human being, I, at least, see it on two levels. On the one hand, each of us is like a speck of dust – so minute, so fragile, that anything can crush it if you place us in the context of the kind of universe we are aware of now. We are really of no account as far as that is concerned. On the other hand, when you think of a human being, he has got within himself a sort of depth, psychological and otherwise, which is such that no amount of knowledge can fill him to the point of being totally satiated – no amount of emotion, no amount of vision, nothing. A human being, small as he is in one way, has a depth, a vastness so great that one can pour into it all knowledge, all love, all beauty, and it drops as though it was in an abyss, and you listen, and you wait for the moment when it will touch the bottom and re-echo, and it never re-echoes. Between these two things, I think, the whole notion of the human being is stretched to the extreme. And I think that, as long as we are not completely, harmoniously fulfilled in body, soul and spirit, there will be hunger. But then we will turn to the kind of things of which we are already aware. We will not, unless we are helped – we will not strive for the unknown. We will say, 'Oh yes, I ate steak and I know that it filled me; I ate sex, I ate music, I ate this, I devoured that'; and then a moment will come later when hunger will be back. And this is the point at which I think Dostoyevsky is right when he says,

'Beauty is ultimately communion with the ultimate beauty, which is God.'

But I have spoken in the first person, not making a universal statement, because I do not think that I can make it. I could tell you that this is the way in which an atheist would put it, an agnostic would put it, a Russian would and so on, but I could not speak with conviction, because it would not be my conviction.

LECTURE 4 – THE SIGNIFICANCE AND PLACE OF UGLINESS

4 NOVEMBER 1982

I think that it is a sad anti-climax to end a series of talks, or lectures, on beauty, by speaking about ugliness, and if ugliness was the last word, I feel it could not be done, and should not be done. But if I speak of the place, or the role, or the significance of ugliness, it is in the context of beauty and because I think that ugliness has a real importance and a real significance – and not only an aesthetic one, but also a moral and a spiritual one.

Yesterday I pointed out the fact that the terminology of beauty was applied since early Christendom to the spiritual realm, and that already the ancient world spoke in the same breath of beauty and goodness. A man was characterised in ancient Greece as beautiful, good and brave in one phrase, in one complex word;[110] and the writings in which the ancient Church embodied its ascetic and mystical teaching were grouped under the term, *Philokalia*,[111] which means 'the love of beauty': not of external beauty, but of a deep essential beauty, both outward and inward.

This sense of beauty led early writers to assert that the

---

[110] Greek: καλὸς κἀγαθός: see final question following Lecture 2.

[111] See footnote 98, Lecture 3.

whole of life is the work of an artist; that each of us is an artist; that the person which we are, or the materials both physical and mental, psychological, spiritual, which go to make up our personality are like the raw materials out of which a sculptor is called to make a statue; that all the work which a person can put into growing to the full stature which is his or hers is the work of an artist, and that the spiritual struggle which begins in the spirit, but also involves and enfolds the psyche and the body, is art of arts.

The final achievement, the most perfect beauty to be achieved and attained to, was described in the words of St Irenaeus when he said, 'A man perfectly fulfilled is the splendour of God.'[112] So that it is not only on the level of the plastic, visual, auditive arts, but in all the realm of human life that beauty or ugliness have got their place and their role.

I quoted yesterday a passage from Dostoyevsky in which he made several points. First of all, he said, 'It is beauty that will save the world.' Beauty is understood by him within the classical tradition as being the convincing power of what is true, the revelation of reality in its real self, unveiled, freed from the ugliness which may be superimposed upon it by our human misunderstandings or by the disfigurement which we bring into the world. But he also insisted that beauty is an enigma, that beauty is not simple, that there is a complexity in beauty that does not allow us simply to distinguish between

[112]   See Lecture 3.

the beautiful and the ugly, as one distinguishes between two colours, between light and darkness and so forth. For him there are two kinds of beauty and, as so often in Dostoyevsky, when he says something it requires a great deal of explanation, because he is not always clear in his own mind what he intends to say; for, having said that there are two kinds of beauty, he goes on, in another passage in his diary, to explain that there are not two kinds of beauty, but there is beauty, but it can be seen in two different ways. One can see with purity of heart, with clarity of mind, or one can see in a confused way, or in a misinterpreting way by projecting upon what is seen – and I am using the word 'seen' in a very general way – projecting on what is seen categories or conditions which are within us.

I have quoted already the story of the spiritual guide who, looking at a prostitute, saw nothing but the glorious beauty with which God had endowed her, whilst his disciples, who were still in the grip of lust and temptation, could not look at her without seeing the ugliness of prostitution in her.[113] In that sense, it is quite definite that beauty is unique, beauty is a whole, and yet there is a problem of the way in which we see it. This applies not only to beauty but to everything in life. Our eye must be clear, our heart must be pure, our intellect must be enlightened, the whole of us must be possessed of integrity and wholeness if we want to see wholeness and integrity around us.

---

[113]   See first question following Lecture 2.

Beauty, then, is not ambiguous in itself, but man is ambiguous. Man is divided within himself, and when I say that, it is so obvious that it does not require much explanation. St Paul in two passages tells us that he feels within himself the tension between two laws: the law of life and a law of corruption;[114] a law, an impulse to live fully, to grow to the full stature, to outgrow all slavery and limitation, and another tendency in him which is inertia and which would be content with being less than a man, be content with grazing instead of living. And he gives another image in another place when he says that there is in him, or in all of us, the new Adam in the image of Christ, and the old Adam in the image of one who has chosen death and corruption.[115] So that when we are confronted with beauty it is not simply a question of recognizing beauty and discerning it from ugliness. There is beauty which is poisonous, not in itself but because of the way we see it, and there is ugliness, objective, outward ugliness that may play a positive role.

The first time I was confronted with this thought was on reading a poem by the French writer, Baudelaire[116] – and I apologise once more for quoting foreigners instead of the appropriate English writers! There is a poem by him called

---

[114] Cf. Romans 7.

[115] Cf. Ephesians 4:20–30

[116] Charles Pierre Baudelaire (1821–1867), poet; also essayist, art critic, and earliest translator of Edgar Allan Poe into French.

The Carcass,[117] where he describes how, walking on a path in the countryside, he came across the carcass, the rotting carcass of a dog, and he describes it crudely, and from there, he moves on to say

And this is, my darling, what you will be.

And then he makes another move, in which he makes us apprehend that that is not the last word. And I think it is very important for us, in all the forms of distortion, all our confrontations with what is wrong, to be able to receive a message from it and to transcend it, to go beyond the ugliness to another vision

Speaking from within my old profession, I would say that, as a doctor, I was very appreciative of all that brought a patient to me, not merely because I was a doctor and he provided my income, but because, if a patient had never felt pain or any kind of discomfort, he would have continued in his condition until he had died of an unknown illness. And the same is true about ugliness when it strikes our attention. From what I have said I would like you to understand that ugliness is not primarily in form, in feature, in shapes. Ugliness, more importantly, is in the way in which we receive a message from what we are confronted with and what happens to us. If I may reiterate the same idea, ugliness

[117]   Charles Beaudelaire, 'A Rotting Carcass' ('Une Charogne'), in *Flowers of Evil* (*Fleurs du Mal*, 1857).

will be in our eye, it will be in our perception. However, there is something to say also about what we would call 'objective ugliness'.

Speaking of human beings, we all react to one another by finding a person ugly or beautiful, but this is true within one cultural setting, within our national setting; what is beautiful for an Englishman may be ugly for an African or for a Chinese person, because the ideal, the canon of beauty is different in the various countries. Thinking of representations of saints, for instance, the English saint is very different from the Greek saint in shape, in colour, in dimensions, and yet both are an attempt at representing the most beautiful thing one can imagine. What can be more beautiful to an English artist than an English face? And what can be more beautiful in the eyes of a Greek, or a Russian than a Greek or Russian shape? Beauty is there all the same; only the form has changed.

There is an interview which was given by a man called Jacques Brel,[118] who was a Belgian-born singer, celebrated throughout the French-speaking world, who died in France of cancer. He was interviewed once about his own ugliness. He was ugly; no one disputed that; he did not dispute it either. And if I may open brackets and close them very quickly, there

---

[118]   See footnote 68, Lecture 2. It has not been possible to identify the specific interview. Brel gave many interviews and often discussed his supposed ugliness.

LECTURE 4 – UGLINESS

is a story in the life of St Vincent de Paul[119] which is very moving. His father, when Vincent was still very young, in his late teens, found him one day standing before a mirror, and he stopped because he did not expect him, ugly as he was, to fall into contemplation of self, and he heard Vincent saying, 'I am far too ugly for men; perhaps God will do with me.' Well, you see, here was an assessment of ugliness according to the conception of what is beautiful or ugly in his time, in his race, in his country, in his circumstances. But there was also a solution to the problem: he was not defeated, he took it as a challenge and asked himself, what does one do when one is like this? And what he did was to achieve one of the greatest pieces of art: saintliness: a man beautifully fulfilled, and a man whose saintliness poured around him and resulted, not only in his time but up to our time, in the good of so many.

When Brel was asked about his own ugliness, he said, 'I think that when one is ugly and still small, one very soon does without feeling that one matters much. It is very difficult to be a beautiful boy of fifteen, both at that age and for the future, because one is centred on one's face and one's appearance. But one who is ugly … oh, for him it is not difficult at all. He walks into a struggle and fights, and fights, turning away from himself and walking into life.' Brel expresses this in the

[119] St Vincent de Paul (1581–1660), French Roman Catholic priest who dedicated himself to serving the poor; venerated as a saint in the Roman Catholic Church and the Anglican Communion; founder of the Congregation of the Mission and of the Daughters of Charity of Saint Vincent de Paul.

same way, although not in the same words, as St Vincent de Paul does.

Then Brel was asked why he mentioned his ugliness quite often in the songs and poetry he wrote; and he said, 'Yes, I speak of it, because I want others to understand that when one is not beautiful, one cannot concentrate one's interests, or anyone else's interests on oneself, but what is left are one's actions and what one can bring and contribute to others.'

I think it is very important to see the creative way in which one can meet with ugliness in all sorts. I do not mean only the ugliness of a face, like St Vincent or Jacques Brel. Many of us – all of us, I suppose – looking at self, can discover that there are within ourselves features which are no joy to us, features which we dislike, features which we despise, features which we feel mar us, prevent us from being the beauty and the revelation of beauty which we could be. However, instead of recoiling, of turning away from it, we can say, 'Yes, how wonderful! It is a frailty within me – yes, it is – but it can teach me to turn away from myself and to busy myself with something which is of much greater importance: life, others, God; one person, or mankind – it does not matter.'

There is also, when it is a psychological or moral frailty in us, another side to this ugliness, because we always perceive frailty, that is defeatedness, in us as being ugly. There is this wonderful passage in St Paul, when he prayed to God that he should be made free of his frailty, whatever it was, and God said to him, 'My grace is enough; My power is made manifest, deploys itself in weakness.' And so St Paul says, 'I will rejoice in my weakness because then all the good will be God's doing.'[120]

And so, again, we can see in ourselves ugly features or weak features, which can give God freedom to act, while if we were possessed of ourselves completely, we could not give Him freedom to act; we would wish, we would determine to act ourselves.

There is another aspect which is almost transcendental, in which our faith and, say, the psychology of Jung could meet quite easily, although we would speak in slightly different terms. It is the fact that we can discover in us ugliness which is not our own personal ugliness, but which is ancestral: qualities, negative qualities, which we have inherited. And again, we can act in two opposite ways. We can turn and say, 'Oh, if I had not had such ancestry, how free I would be to be a glory to myself and to God!' Or instead of this we could take a quite different line and say, 'I have inherited not only a weakness, a frailty or evil qualities, but a task. If what I have inherited I can transform, I can transfigure, I can make into something new, then I will not only have put myself right, I will also have done something for those who have preceded me; I will not transmit further, qualities which will make them hated or feared.'

All this implies, in a way, that ugliness, personal or

---

[120]   2 Corinthians 12:9–10.

collective, is something which we must face in ourselves, in our society, in mankind, in a creative, in a daring and in an inspired manner. It is our task; it is something which we must learn from and overcome. But then ugliness also may appear to us in frightening terms. I have quoted already to you the attitude of Edgar Poe[121] to what was beautiful and what was ugly. To him, as he demonstrates in two of his essays,[122] anything which is not exactly on the scale of man is frightening and, therefore, repulsive, and cannot be termed beauty, but horror, fear, dread. He gives examples: a thunderstorm; a storm on the sea; a horizon too vast; anything that breaks or destroys his sense of security and protectedness is ugly and is evil. And he gives us in these two essays an atrocious image of what he imagines to be a domain or a garden: something which is small enough for him never to feel that he is unprotected by the end of the horizon, unprotected by the limits in which he lives. This is a cowardly approach to life. If we want to face life we must face it, as I have said before, as a chaos that is a mysterious reality full and pregnant with possibilities which have not yet emerged and which, when they do emerge, may frighten us if we are not prepared to grow as great as they are. Ugliness and beauty, in that respect, claim from us greatness, and we

[121]   See footnote 10, Lecture 1.

[122]   Edgar Allan Poe, *Landor's Cottage*, and *The Domain of Arnheim*: see Lecture 1.

LECTURE 4 – UGLINESS

cannot face ugliness unless we stand tall on the ground, unless we are prepared to look at it daringly and take the risk of life and death, but not accept defeat and humiliation.

Ugliness may well be a quite legitimate description of reality, by which I mean that at times art, whether it is poetry, prose or visual or other arts, has got to confront us with the ugliness or horror of life. And again, it is a cowardly thing on our part to shrink away from ugliness and to hope that nothing but harmony, beauty or simply something neutral enough not to frighten us will confront us. I remember a grandmother who read stories to her grandchildren and she always changed the end, because the end was always to be an apotheosis, it had to be sweet and beautiful and … Ah! I see someone in the audience laugh! I must say it was not my grandmother; it was someone else's grandmother!

Now, we must be prepared to see the ugliness, to look into it deeply. A physician has got to look at the horror and ugliness of illness and of pain, and *we* have got to have the courage to do this too. For a year and a half after the war, I was in charge of people coming back from German concentration camps. It was an ugly sight, it was a heart-rending sight, but it had to be looked into as deeply as possible because only by looking into it with all one's mind, all one's heart, all one's being, at the risk, in a way, of being deeply wounded, could one hope to do something useful. We are unwilling to look at what happened, or happens still in concentration camps, in war, in illness, in hunger, in suffering of all types: we must

121

have the courage to do it. We acquire a certain courage to do it in an indirect way, in a novel, because we know that the chances are that the tension will be resolved; in a play, or in the cinema, because we feel that at any moment, if the terror is too great, the horror is too deep, we will be able to feel the armrests of our seats and say, 'That happens to them, not to me; it is all right.'

'It is all right' is a terrible phrase. We may take care not to say that, because we are hypocritical enough, all of us, or careful enough not to place ourselves before a judgement seat, but – yes – we are safe. The book is too frightening: I can close it. The film or the play is too horrible: I become aware of being outside of it. Well, we must learn not to do this.

A certain number of years ago, I gave a talk about hunger in India, after the gruelling experience of what I had seen there in the sixties. I spoke with all the passion of which I am capable, and at times I *can* put passion into what I say! At the end of the service, because it was in a church, there were intercessions for the hungry; then there was a collection and, as I was standing at the west door with the vicar, a sweet little old woman came up to me, extended her hand and said, 'Thank you, dear Father, for a most entertaining evening.' Well, not being English, that is having no inhibitions to being rude, I said to her, 'I hope that you gave more than a shilling for your entertainment!' Well, you know, she had managed to escape it, though she had seen it happening, in the newspaper, perhaps, or on television. 'Yes, it is over there. I have to look up India on the map, I cannot remember where it is, it is some sort of triangle somewhere to the right on the map. But it is over there, it is not us; they are so different. And then, you know, they have been hungry for so many centuries, they are used to it. That is all right. It would not be all right for us.' You are imagining that I am just giving caricatures. I am not: it is exactly what I have heard said in one situation or another. When I speak of horror, such as occurred in the Soviet Union for example, I am told, 'Oh, yes, but it cannot happen to us, we are not Russians!'

So, there is a message which ugliness brings to us: it is a challenge. It says to us, 'The world in which you live, and which you have made, and which you sustain by your indifference, your cowardice, your softness is ugly, monstrous, and there are millions of people who pay the cost of it. Look at it!' In that sense perhaps, ugliness – with the implied possibility of redemption, of change, of transfiguration – is more essential than the sight of harmony and beauty, because ugliness must give us the ability to discern, to see, to understand, to be horrified and never to come to peace with the things it shows us.

And then there is also the representation of ugliness, in all the ways in which it is represented when what we represent is ugly. Anger is ugly, cowardice is ugly and so many other things. I remember someone, in a fit of anger, by chance seeing his face in a mirror. Anger fell off at once because it

123

was so ugly that he said, 'But … I cannot allow myself to look like this!' If we could look at ourselves a little bit more when we are angry, when we are greedy, when we are resentful, when we are lusting and so forth, we would probably say, 'Is this really what I am?' (It is for a split second.) 'Is this really what there is in me? Can I accept to be like this? Because my face was not that way a minute ago: if it is that way now it is because my content has reached my features and given them this monstrous, revolting shape.'

But then there is also evil, and evil which, in terms of art, can penetrate and use art. I gave you a quotation yesterday from Dostoyevsky,[123] in which there are several elements. The first one is that in the turmoil of life, in the grip of tragedy, we long for equipoise, for harmony, for stillness, for serenity, and this leads us to create the kind of art which brings out all the beauty of which we can become aware, not only intellectually, rationally, but which can well up from the depth of our being. It is not at every moment that this is possible. You may not know, but I will share a secret with you, that for three centuries Russia was under the Tartar yoke; it was for three centuries submitted to great violence and cruelty. If you look at the art of this epoch, suffering is not depicted in it. What is depicted in it is all the beauty that could be remembered or that was seen in the ways of people, because people needed an anchor in hope.

[123]   See footnote 24, Lecture 1.

LECTURE 4 – UGLINESS

But when the Tartar yoke came to an end, then the artists began to give images of what suffering and tragedy are. You find suffering and tragedy in the works of a man like Rublev,[124] but you do not find them fifty or one hundred years before. It would have been intolerable, unbearable in the face of actual horror, to be confronted with nothing but a picture of horror unresolved, because at that moment, it could not be resolved. The resolution was in showing that, at the heart of it, beauty survived, that in spite of it beauty was accessible, that, however ugly things were, there could be beauty.

In the experience that I have had in that one year and a half, eighteen months or so of work with people that had come from concentration camps, the thing that struck me was that, apart from the horror which they conveyed to me (I was treating their bodies, but I was also in charge of rehabilitating them for life as best I could.), I heard so much about the courage, the greatness of heart, the patience, the generosity and so many other wonderful qualities which they or their companions in captivity had shown, because these were the only things that made it possible for them to survive. Within ugliness there were sparks of harmony and beauty within one person, or for one moment, or for a short period, or in one situation, and that was the salvation of many.

[124] St Andrei Rublev, born in the 1360s, died about 1430 in Moscow, considered to be one of the greatest mediaeval Russian painters of Orthodox icons and frescos. Commemorated 4 July.

But evil can touch something more tragically perhaps: it may touch the good itself. Ugliness can be like a serpent in the grass, like poison in a fruit, like death in one of those flowers that close upon a victim and digest it. Dostoyevsky, in the same quotation, having indicated to us that the struggle, the pain, the difficulty of life, the tragedy of life, brought to the fore a longing for harmony and wholeness, integrity and beauty, says that another thing which is tragic is that, when life is made of nothing but contentment, when there is no directedness, no intensity, no struggle, no aim in life, then a new hunger pervades the people, a hunger to fill the place which intensity would fill; and then horrible, monstrous forms begin to appear.

I will give you one quotation from Dostoyevsky again. He says, in the words of one of his characters:

Oh, my friends, you cannot imagine what sadness and anger seize your whole soul when a great idea long revered by you as sacred is taken up by bunglers and dragged out into the street to just such fools as themselves, as you suddenly encounter it now in the free market, unrecognizable, filthy, stood up absurdly at an angle, without proportion, without harmony – a plaything in the hands of stupid children.[125]

This is something which he points out more than once:

[125] Fyodor M. Dostoyevsky, *Demons* (Бесы, 1872).

126

LECTURE 4 – UGLINESS

that when society or individuals have nothing to strive for, are satiated, then society will fall, singly or collectively, into a kind of anguish, and will invent in itself anguish if necessary, seek out some sort of ideal, some sort of thing to strive towards of extreme surfeit of pleasure. Not only would it not value what had been enjoyed, but would consciously turn from the direct path, exciting in itself alien tendencies, unhealthy, disharmonic, monstrous sometimes. Now this is the point at which moral judgement plays a decisive role in discernment in beauty. And when I say moral judgement, I do not mean pre-conceived principles that would rule out certain forms of art in favour of other forms of art. I mean the perceptiveness that will allow a person to say, 'This is degrading; this makes me small; this is below me; this is unworthy of my human stature; this is something that quenches the spirit; this is something which is contrary to life; this is corruption; this is death; this is vile.' This is a moral principle in the sense that it cannot be deduced simply from the consideration of the object. Pornography is the name which I could attach to it to make a shortcut and, unfortunately, in the kind of society in which we live, which is easy and where the struggle for life is very limited, we are very easily made prisoners, caught by this kind of acceptance of what should be repulsive to us because it is a negation of wholeness and of dignity.

Here is a definition of the consumer society, or high

standard of living, which was given by John Kenneth Galbraith[126] in a book called *The Affluent Society*:[127]

> *What is called a high standard of living consists in considerable measure in arrangements for avoiding muscular effort, for increasing sensual pleasure and enhancing caloric intake above any conceivable nutritional requirement.*

When we speak of this intake, it means not only food: it means the greed implied in it, and the greed goes far beyond; it goes into lust, it goes into possessiveness, it goes into the lowering of all standards in the acceptance that we are not called to be as great as God (as Angelus Silesius[128] put it), that we are like fungi on this earth or, as someone else put it, like a cancer on nature, on a world which we should make noble and great.

Now, I would like to conclude with two quotations, and perhaps redeem myself a little for having quoted all the time foreign writers. I have given a little thought to it. I have recognised yesterday that it is my ignorance which is mainly the cause of it. But when I asked myself, 'Was it only

---

[126] John Kenneth Galbraith (1908-2006), Canadian-born economist, public official, and diplomat, and a leading proponent of twentieth-century American liberalism.

[127] John Kenneth Galbraith, *The Affluent Society* (1958).

[128] Angelus Silesius (c 1624–1677), born Johann Scheffler and also known as Johann Angelus Silesius, German Roman Catholic priest and physician, known as a mystic and religious poet.

ignorance?' I remembered that when I began to collect my data, I thought it would do you no harm to be confronted with writers and names which perhaps are less familiar to you than Keats, Shakespeare or Yeats. This was really brought to my mind a few years ago. I spoke in one of the universities to the department of psychiatry and psychology. There were only teaching personnel and research students. I mentioned the names of Nietzsche and of Pascal, and at the end of my talk I was asked who they were! I returned the compliment by saying, 'Could any one of you enlighten your friend?' There was no one to enlighten their friend! So, having poured out names on you, perhaps I have incited you to have a look at – well, at an encyclopaedia!

Now, here is a quotation from Keats:[129]

Beauty is truth, truth beauty, – that is all
Ye know on earth, and all ye need to know.[130]

And another:

A thing of beauty is a joy for ever;
Its loveliness increases; it will never
Pass into nothingness, …[131]

---

[129] See footnote 107, Lecture 3.

[130] From Keats' 'Ode on a Grecian Urn' (1820).

[131] From Keats' 'Endymion' (1818).

What I wanted to convey in these talks is that beauty, ugliness, the totality of life has a deep, a decisive meaning; it matters; and that if we cannot reason things out, if we are not philosophers or theologians, if we have not got access to the highest process of the mind, there is yet one way in which we are confronted and challenged by life and in which we can confront life, challenge life and resolve life: by assessing ugliness and beauty on a basis which is spiritual, which is moral, which is not simply an aesthetic judgement of form, but an understanding of what it brings to us: then choose life and build it, even if it costs us our life!

I am sorry. I am a preacher by nature, so I probably have done it again, and I apologise to you!

QUESTIONS

In The Brothers Karamazov *of Dostoyevsky, the young monk, kneeling by the rotting body of the old monk said, 'What a shame if people should think he was not a saint,' and then he looked again and he saw the marriage, with him, smiling. I think this is the contrast; he did not ignore the rotting of the corpse, he knelt there, you know, sharing.* [132]

[132] Fyodor M. Dostoyevsky, *The Brothers Karamazov* (Братья Карамазовы, 1880): In Part III, Book VII, Chapter 4, Alyosha, the young monk, praying beside the corpse of the dead elder Zosima, has a vision of the elder present at a wedding feast.

LECTURE 4 – UGLINESS

I am very grateful for what you say. You can transcend the vision of ugliness, if you look at it and look deeply. If you remain on the surface it will only be the smell of the carcass, but you can look deeper. If I may make a short comparison, there is in Edgar Poe a story (I cannot remember its name) in which a young man goes to the cemetery and re-opens the grave of his beloved one.[133] If you compare it to Baudelaire's poem, *The Carcass*, you will see the difference. Baudelaire sees the ugliness, recognizing in it what it is, draws the ultimate and horrible conclusion and outgrows it, while in Edgar Poe it ends in a sort of ghoulish and sinister vision that leads nowhere. And it is because of his attitude.

I do not quite know how relevant this is, but it keeps coming into my mind to ask you if you know about the work of Wilhelm Reich,[134] and how that would fit in with thinking in terms of ugliness and beauty. He was thinking about people's bodies and the way they hold themselves. (This is a very simple explanation.) He considered there was an essential person within whatever misshape that person had become, and he worked on the actual body of that person to sort

---

[133] Perhaps Metropolitan Anthony is referring to Edgar Allan Poe's *The Black Cat* (1843).

[134] Wilhelm Reich (1897–1957), controversial Austrian physician and psychoanalyst, a member of the second generation of analysts after Sigmund Freud; died in prison in the USA.

of bring it back into its balance. I wonder how far you would agree that there is in each person a sort of unique person there, which can be brought back into being.

I believe passionately, as I do most things, that in each of us there is a person who is unique and unrepeatable. There is a passage in the Book of Revelation in which we are told that, in the Kingdom, each of us will be possessed of a name which no one knows but God and he to whom it is given.[135] You may know that, in Hebrew tradition, and in early Christian tradition, the name was not simply an appellation, a way of distinguishing Peter from Mary; it was meant to be a total, an ultimate expression of the person. This indicates that in the Kingdom every one of us will relate to God in a way which is absolutely unrepeatable and unique. And this is there, already now; it will not be created of a sudden, but it is veiled, it is distorted. We ourselves cannot see our own face, but God can. I quoted you this phrase of a Russian bishop who says: 'When God looks at us he does not see the achievements or virtues which are not there, but he sees the beauty which is there and cannot be erased.' In that sense, there is absolute uniqueness: no one can be replaced. And if you think of what will be, say mankind or the cosmos in eternity, each of us is like a small stone in a mosaic: it may be a very

---

[135] Revelation 2:17.

small stone, but if you remove one stone the mosaic will gradually fall to pieces.

Now, as regards acting through the body upon the whole person, there is no doubt that we are not a soul encaged in a body, imprisoned in a body. A human being is an incarnate reality, in which the spiritual, the psychological and the physical are profoundly intertwined in much the same way as fire or heat can pervade metal. And all the ascetic traditions of not only Christianity, but of all religions, teach us that one can affect not only our mental content but our spiritual destiny, free ourselves inwardly by acting upon the body. So this would be a particular way, or a particular case, but the principle, I think would be recognised universally.

Archbishop, if I could take you to the question of the depiction of horror and bestiality and immorality in art: some of the artists working during and after the First World War, such as Max Beckman[136] and George Grosz,[137] depicted, if you like, man's inhumanity to man in most vivid terms. Does that reduce the value of those as works of art, or are they redeemed somehow by a further moral lesson that they had to teach us?

[136] Max Beckmann (1884–1950), German painter, draftsman, printmaker, sculptor and writer, associated in the 1920s with the New Objectivity (Neue Sachlichkeit) group.

[137] George Grosz, born Georg Ehrenfried Groß (1893–1959), German artist, a prominent member of the Berlin Dada and New Objectivity group, known for his caricatural drawings and paintings of Berlin life in the 1920s.

You know, it is not the content of a poem or a painting that makes it good or bad. There are extremely good feelings that are expressed in very bad poetry, and the same would apply to all forms of art. I think that there are several approaches. If you take Dostoyevsky's approach, he would say that to depict horror, without showing how it is resolved, is bad art. A painting should represent, say, tragedy, in such a way that you see the light coming, dawning. I do not believe this is true. I think what Dostoyevsky would like is to be shown a picture of horror and, instead of having himself to draw the conclusion and bring out the meaning and so forth, that it should be done for him beforehand! I do believe that to be confronted in an undiluted way with ugliness and horror is something which we must accept. But we must not imagine that there is nothing more to it: and that is the risk or the danger of pictures that represent nothing but the horror, because the majority of people will be unable to disentangle themselves from the feeling of horror, which this picture, or this poem, or whatever it is, evokes.

From a pedagogical point of view there is a point in showing within the horror a key of harmony, a possibility of resolution. You know, I spent five years in the war, and I have very definite views about it. I do not find it a lovely experience; I do not find war a desirable experience. I have seen ugliness in it in plenty, as all the men or women of my generation have seen. So I am not being romantic about it, but what I would say is that I have never seen so far – I mean within those five years – ever a monstrous situation that did not call out something in one man or another, or in the way in which people related, that tended to redeem the horror, that showed that even within the horror something can happen.

I would like to give you a couple of examples, which are not taken from my experience at all because lyricism is always too near to exhibitionism.

After the war, in one of the concentration camps, was found a prayer, written by a Jew, on a torn piece of wrapping paper; I do not remember it by heart, and I cannot quote it in full, but those of you who are foolish enough to read my books can find it in *Living Prayer*, quoted from a German newspaper. In substance, it said this:

> *Lord, when you will come to judge the earth, do not look at the cruelty, the violence, the vileness of the people who tormented us so cruelly, and do not allow our suffering to be their condemnation; but look at all the fortitude, the patience, the courage, the comradeship which all these horrors have brought to the fore in our midst, and take all that as a redemption for what they have done.*[138]

I could not say that, and I doubt that *you* could say that from the comfort of our present-day life, but this man had a right to say it.

---

[138] Metropolitan Anthony of Sourozh, *Living Prayer* (1966).

I can quote another man, who was an older friend of mine, who spent four years in a concentration camp. When he came back I met him in the street and I said to him, 'What have you brought back from there?' And he said, 'Agony of mind.' I said, 'Have you lost your faith?' And he said, 'No, but as long as I was the victim of all the brutality which was poured upon us, I knew I had power to forgive. I could turn to God and say, "Lord, do not condemn these men, because in Thy name I have forgiven." Now I am free, and I do not know whether those men who tormented us in such a way have understood what they had been doing, have repented, have changed. And when I turn to God and say, "God, oh God, save them!" I have always an anguish within myself as though God was saying to me, "What right have you to pray now for them? – you are not suffering."'

You know: that this kind of attitude could be born in this Jew, in this Russian Orthodox (and I could go on quoting examples) is something which could help when we are confronted with a picture, either in words or colour or line or otherwise, of horror, because too many people will not be able to see and discern.

Do you consider it necessary for great art to have a moral content?

Yes, I do. That is, I do believe that art must have a content, and that this content, when it is presented to someone who will perceive it, should be such that the spectator or the listener should become greater than he is, and not less than he is. Of course, I start with my preconceptions, but you asked me a question in the first person and I said, 'Yes, indeed!' Otherwise it is anti-art, it is the exploitation, the profanation of art, it is a rape of form. It is a betrayal of a means of communication in order to destroy what should be built.